The Politics of Unity

The Politics of Unity

An Invitation to the High Road

Michael Cuddehe

Three Worlds Press
Fairfield

ISBN: 978-0-9975771-0-5 Print
ISBN: 978-0-9975771-1-2 eBook
Library of Congress Control Number: 2016911158

Three Worlds Press
PO Box 168
Fairfield, IA 52556

Contents

For those who would create a better world

Acknowledgments

The Politics of Unity has been percolating for 25 years. Over that time, countless people and influences have come to bear on my thinking and eventually, on this finished product. To all of them I extend my heartfelt thanks. In particular, I wish to acknowledge the contributions of the following people:

Dr. John Hagelin, Bob Roth, Kingsley Brooks, Mike Tompkins, Bob Oates, Rob Stowe, Elaine Redding, Sally Rosenfeld and Gerry Geer at the Natural Law Party; my campaign managers Brenda Narducci and Jane Allon, and campaign supporters, Bob Rutt, Fred Swartz, Marian O'Sullivan, and the many volunteers who pitched in for ballot access; the rest of the '96 Iowa NLP slate, Rogers Badgett, Michael Dimick, Fred Gratzon, Peter Lamoureux and Jay Marcus. Also Walter Reifslager, Matthew Beaufort and Elizabeth Brazell for their early encouragement and support; readers of the rough draft of this book, Bob Bunshaft, Barry Ross, Laury Sluser, Sheila Ross and Ellen Metropole; Bernie Nevas for his consistent support; Stuart Bluestone for his invaluable suggestions; and my beloved wife and relentless editor, Jane, who is entirely responsible for proper grammar and clarity of expression.

The most important and valuable influence of all has been the comprehensive vision and teaching of Maharishi Mahesh Yogi, who gave me the wisdom of integration of life, and the tools to put that wisdom into practice.

PART 1

Principles: An Invitation to the High Road

1

Introduction

The first draft of *The Politics of Unity* was written in 1990 in Malibu, California. The essential ideas were all there, but the time was not yet right for publication. Since then, we have endured a long downward spiral of increasing polarization, and simultaneous degradation of our political process.

It appears we may be approaching the nadir of this destructive cycle. We are headed either for a breakdown of order, or a general awakening to the need for a higher path. I now feel the time is ripe for the insights and solutions offered in *The Politics of Unity*.

The current version, written in Fairfield, Iowa, the home of the Natural Law Party, is a refinement and condensation of those seminal thoughts put to paper in 1990.

Personally, a great deal has transpired between 1990 and 2016. I participated in the Natural law Party campaigns of 1994 and 1996, as a candidate for U.S. Representative in

Iowa's First District. My opponent was Jim Leach, one of a previous generation of politicians who believed in the principles of *loyal* opposition and public *service.* Jim demonstrated to me that it is possible to be an honorable person in public life and truly serve the public interest, even when those around you are not and do not.

During those campaigns I became familiar with the major issues—which with a few notable exceptions, have not changed substantively—and with our political process, which unfortunately *has* changed, and not for the better. The Natural Law Party's approach to problem solving also opened my awareness to the importance of finding balanced solutions to meet the needs of the *whole* of society.

In 2001 I began writing the quarterly political and economic newsletter, *Risk & Opportunity*. This task has required me to continuously monitor, absorb and report on market, economic, political and geopolitical developments and trends, resulting in a fine attunement to the state of affairs in all of these areas.

In the process of writing *Risk & Opportunity* I have gained a clear perception of the destructive forces driving the fragmentation of our society, and a clear vision of the actions needed to mitigate those forces. Moreover, I have become keenly aware of the magnitude of the collective challenge presented by our dramatically expanding technological power, and the most important steps needed to enable us to meet that challenge.

The various ideas, values, principles, processes and policies constituting a *Politics of Unity* are presented in short essays and organized in two Parts. This book is envisioned as a handbook to be shared, referenced and discussed.

Part One: An Invitation to the High Road, addresses the fundamental reality and implications of our common position and interdependence on planet Earth, and presents guiding principles for a political process to promote honest debate, social cohesion and the best possible policy outcomes.

Part Two: Getting From Here to There, identifies the key roadblocks to an elevated political process, and presents policies and procedures for ensuring constructive process and accountability for public officials.

Part One is philosophy; Part Two is application. Chapter 35 is where philosophy meets application, summarizing *The Politics of Unity* in action. A separate volume is envisioned to apply the principles of *The Politics of Unity* to policy in all areas of public interest.

This format was chosen for two reasons. One, our ability to absorb long-form publications has become seriously constrained by Internet browsing, which has had the effect of dramatically reducing the attention span of the average reader to something less than a goldfish—approximately 8 seconds.[1] Two, presenting the essence of the ideas in short essays allows for easy reference and application across the partisan divide, a primary objective of the book.

The ideas presented in this book are well considered, offering an elevated approach to political process based on the core principles of balance and unity. We are not condemned to continue on the path of endless conflict until the worst happens. We can pivot in this time of great consequence to a higher path.

Notes

1. *Attention Span Statistics*, StatisticBrain.com, http://www.statisticbrain.com/attention-span-statistics/ (June 15, 2016).

2

The Value of Simplicity

> Any intelligent fool can make things bigger, more complex, and more violent. It takes a touch of genius—and a lot of courage—to move in the opposite direction.
>
> —*Albert Einstein*

Much of the end product of our political process—our public policy—is convoluted and opaque. A good deal of that convoluted output is deliberate, in order to hide the true aim of the policy. Much of it is also simply a result of a process that has lost its way due to neglect.

We argue endlessly about policy, but we don't think much about process. If the public demanded clear and straightforward presentation of ideas and honest debate on the merits, our politics and our policy would be light years ahead of their current debilitated state.

Simplicity in presentation communicates. Initially it takes

more time and effort to develop a clean and simple presentation of an idea, or an objective, but that extra time and effort up front pays dividends down the road.

Simplicity in service to political process and policy formation will yield clarity of purpose, transparency in process and efficiency in application; and it will promote service over exploitation from our representatives and officials.

3

On Transcendence

No problem can be solved from the same level of consciousness that created it.

—*Albert Einstein*

For anyone interested in a better life, in making a contribution to a better world, or in solving problems of any kind, transcendence is a key concept.

For the purposes of this volume, we will take the definition of *transcending* as "going beyond," as in the philosophical definition of "going beyond some philosophical concept or limit."

In order to solve a problem or conflict, we must go beyond, or transcend the problem to gain a broader and more comprehensive perspective—a perspective of greater commonality, shared values, or underlying unity. This is the essence of *The Politics of Unity*.

In the areas of political process, public policy formation and governance, transcendence has profound implications. By employing the principle of transcendence, surface level conflicts can systematically be resolved, promoting productive policy and governance in service to the greatest good. This method can be applied to virtually all areas of public policy, including hot-button issues such as taxes, abortion and gun rights.

A prerequisite to the application of this concept is the *willingness* to transcend conflict and seek a broader framework. The narrower the framework, the more binary the choices appear to be, and the more difficult it is to achieve compromise. As perspective broadens, areas of commonality come into view and resolution can often become a win-win, instead of either-or, and win-lose.

Compromise is the life blood of democracy. Political process and governance break down when opposing parties refuse to do so—as we have seen in recent years in America. Compromise is enabled by the transcendence of superficial conflict to expand context and identify areas of commonality upon which solutions can be found. We can restore order to our political process by electing representatives with a demonstrated willingness and ability to do so.

For those interested in a more in-depth treatment of transcendence and its implications for personal and societal development, there is an excellent book on the subject entitled, simply, *Transcendence*[1] by Dr. Norman Rosenthal.

Wikipedia also has a good series of sites on transcendence, accessed here[2] and here.[3]

Notes

1. Rosenthal, Norman. 2012. *Transcendence: Healing and Transformation Through Transcendental Meditation.* New York, NY. Penguin.
2. *Transcendence,* Wikipedia, https://en.wikipedia.org/wiki/Transcendence (May 18, 2016).
3. *Transcendence_(philosophy),* Wikipedia, https://en.wikipedia.org/wiki/Transcendence_(philosophy) (May 18,2016).

4

Our Position

Human life on planet Earth is a miracle. In an incomprehensibly vast universe, almost entirely inhospitable to life as we know it, our presence here is a miracle. We humans find ourselves perched on the outskirts of a galaxy spinning in the void of interstellar space, on a planet *just* the right distance from our sun, with *just* the right shaped orbit around that sun, with *just* the right density, and all the necessary elements to generate and sustain organic life.

If we were just a little further away from the sun, it would be too cold; a little closer, too hot. If our orbit around the sun were more elliptical, it would be alternately too hot and too cold. And this discussion barely touches the surface of the vast array of interdependent forces on every level, from universal to particle, that are perfectly balanced to make life on Earth possible.

One doesn't have to be religious to stand in awe of our

existence. We only need to take a little time to stand back from the relentless demands and distractions of daily life to contemplate the context of our existence, and the great mystery of the fact that we *do* exist.

If we took more time to contemplate the miracle of our existence here, and our utter dependence on planet Earth, how improbable it is, and just how rare and precious this planet is to us, we might take a little more care in how we treat it. We might be more deliberate and thoughtful in how we organize ourselves to pursue our needs and desires, more careful in how we allocate and exploit our natural resources, and how we manage and process our waste products. We might make more serious efforts to come together to take better care of our one and only home and sanctuary in an inhospitable universe.

For those inclined to delve deeper into this topic, Stephen Hawking and Leonard Mlodinow published an elegant materialistic review of the array of forces enabling human life on planet Earth entitled *The Grand Design.*[1]

Notes

1. Hawking, Stephen and Leonard Mlodinow. 2010. *The Grand Design*. New York, NY. Bantam Books.

5

The Choices We Make

Every man walks the path that he has made.
—*Rig Veda*

Our political process has been mired in the tangled undergrowth of the low road for so long that we seem to have forgotten there is any other choice. Regardless of our forgetfulness, the road we take is a choice—an ongoing choice we make individually and collectively every day.

We are not the creators of our existence here on planet Earth. That we exist at all has come to be, either by divine decree according to the religious, or by happenstance and natural law according to the materialists.

But we *are* the creators of our *experience* here. The extent to which we suffer or prosper is, for the most part, the direct consequence of our individual and collective choices.

How we go about our affairs, how we treat each other and

our planet, what we value and what we don't, the actions we take based on those values and our responses to the conditions we have created as they are reflected back to us, are all choices we make. Those choices have direct impact on the quality of our life experience.

Lost in the disorder reigning in public life is the reality that we are the creators of this disorder, and that we have the power to create a better experience. There won't be any *deus ex machina* that will sweep in to save us. We must choose to make the necessary changes ourselves.

6

The Role of Natural Law

The values defining and guiding a society are grounded in culture, which develops regionally over centuries, and normally changes at a glacial pace. Culture is embodied in the institutions of a society; it is imprinted on the individual citizens of a society as they develop, in a process of *enculturation.*

Culture provides boundaries and values guiding the daily life and trajectory of society; it is the touchstone of stability; it provides a platform for consensus and adjudication of disputes; it is the foundation of social identity, and a moral guide for individual life.

Culture is deeply rooted, emanating ultimately from the natural law of each region.

Put simply, we humans are an integral part of nature, which itself manifests according to natural law. As a part of the natural world, we are subject to and governed by natural law. If we violate natural law, we will pay a penalty. If we organize and live our lives according to natural law, we will "live long and prosper."

The role of a Creator aside (one can make the case with and without), all creation manifests according to the dynamic interaction of an intricate web of consistent forces, constantly adapting to maintain balance between and among the myriad forces in play.

When contemplating this awe-inspiring creation, it is natural to consider how the force of nature is driving the dynamics of human society, and how we might best organize our affairs to be in alignment with this force, not against it.

Natural law has a long history in Western political philosophy, extending from the Greek & Roman philosophers through the major Western philosophers to the framers of the U.S. Constitution, and is a fundamental concept of the Eastern Vedic and Taoist traditions. Wikipedia has a good summary of natural law in the various philosophical traditions available here.[1]

A contemporary application of the principle of natural law, drawn from both Eastern and Western traditions in political thought, is the Natural Law Party, which was founded in 1992, and has participated in elections in over 74 countries.

The Natural Law Party motto is "prevention-oriented government and conflict-free politics," meaning that our government should be working to prevent problems from arising by organizing society in harmony with principles of natural law, and by identifying nascent imbalances so that they can be resolved before they become big problems.

The meaning of "conflict free politics" is that balanced opposition and vigorous debate are not "conflict." They in fact create a vital and healthy dynamic that informs good policy decisions and governance. Opposition becomes conflict only when it is "unbalanced" (i.e. dishonest, disrespectful, myopic, intransigent).

The NLP promoted solutions to public policy issues across the board including health, economy, education, agriculture, energy and environment, defense, and culture war issues such as taxes, abortion, gun control, capital punishment, family values and minority rights. It promoted the practice of Transcendental Meditation for its proven value in the reduction of stress, a modern epidemic, and for its scientifically validated effects on personal life, including improved mental and physical health, greater success at school and work, improved social interaction, and the ability of individuals to give expression to their full potential (self-actualization).[2]

A self-realized individual, giving expression to his/her full potential, will spontaneously live and operate in harmony with natural law, becoming an asset to society. Brick by brick, a society composed of such self-actualized individuals will spontaneously become an ideal society.

The Natural Law Party platform is available online at Natural-Law.org.[3] Further information on Transcendental Meditation is available at TM.org, and information on applications of TM to disadvantaged populations at DavidLynchFoundation.org.

Notes

1. *Natural law*, Wikipedia, https://en.wikipedia.org/wiki/Natural_law (August 15, 2016).
2. *Research on meditation*, TM.org, http://www.tm.org/research-on-meditation (August 15, 2016)
3. *Platform*, Natural Law Party, http://www.natural-law.org/platform/index.html (May 18,2016).

7

Balance

The Greek term *philosophia* translates as "love of wisdom." Originally, philosophy was the pursuit of wisdom regarding the nature of existence, and a practical inquiry into the source of the inherent order in creation, or natural law, that provides the foundation of life, and guidance for living a "good life."

As a fundamental philosophical consideration, the concept of natural law is central to virtually all political philosophies. And while there are different perspectives on the application of natural law to social organization, some basic principles of natural law can nevertheless provide *universal* guidance and practical utility for political process and policy considerations.

First and foremost is the central principle of natural law—*balance*. This principle is apparent in many natural phenomena.

The centrifugal force of revolving galaxies threatens to tear them apart, but the gravitational pull of their central black holes holds them together. These are opposing forces in *balance.* In ecology, species overpopulation brings predation and/or starvation into play to restore *balance.* In economics, excess supply or demand creates price movement to restore *balance* between supply and demand.

We will not "live long and prosper" if we favor the centrifugal over the gravitational force, and our economy will suffer if we favor the supply over the demand. If opposing forces are respected and embraced—each for what they have to offer—they will work in harmony, creating balance and long-term stability.

If the principle of *balance* becomes central to our political thinking, our policies will reflect the intention to meet the needs of all interest groups. It will be natural to review the effectiveness of policies over time and make adjustments as necessary to maintain balance. In this way we will gain optimal results from policy, and maintain systemic stability.

If, however, we deliberately create imbalance by benefiting one interest group at the expense of others, the whole of society will suffer, and the forces inherent in nature will eventually act to restore balance. *The longer an imbalance is maintained, the greater the eventual restorative force will be.* Nature's remedies can be harsh. Revolution and economic collapse are extreme examples.

An excellent example of this principle is the disparity in wealth and income between the upper tier and the great majority of Americans, which is the result of tax and regulatory changes over the past 30 years designed to favor our wealthiest citizens.

This imbalance has created deep and widespread resentment, resulting in the rise of populist candidates to threaten the established order in Washington. Socialist Bernie Sanders has split the Democrat Party, and Fascist leaning Donald Trump has actually secured the Republican nomination for President.

This issue has now become critical and needs to be addressed immediately. We would do well to examine where else we have created imbalances, especially on a large scale, and address them deliberately, rather than waiting for nature to impose a solution.

8

Dharma

Dharma is an Eastern term, which does not have a direct English translation, but is most simply understood as "right action." Buddhists take a proprietary attitude toward the term, using the phrase "*the* dharma," meaning living in accord with the principles of Buddhism. A broader and more precise definition is provided by Maharishi Mahesh Yogi:

> Dharma is that invincible force of nature which upholds existence. It maintains evolution and forms the very basis of cosmic life. It supports all that is helpful for evolution and discourages all that is opposed to it.[1]

Dharma is essentially not a moralistic term, but a broad and basic concept which includes one's place in society, one's vocation, one's actions and values. Dharma is balanced living. Dharma is naturalness. Dharma is righteousness, a natural and deeply rooted righteousness emanating from living life in harmony with the laws of nature.

Dharma is a useful concept when considering issues of policy and political process. It embraces the entire field of life and promotes the understanding that there is a way of being in the world; a way of structuring society; a way of acting, both individually and collectively, that is inherently in harmony with natural law, and which will yield beneficial results for the entire society.

The concept of dharma is a comprehensive way of thinking about natural law. Any activity or policy that promotes personal evolution and the progress of society is dharma; any that is opposed to these values is "a-dharma," opposed to dharma. National defense is dharma. A war of aggression is a-dharma. Criminal justice is dharma. For-profit prisons are a-dharma. Freedom and self-determination is dharma. Slavery is a-dharma. Economic exchange is dharma. Theft is a-dharma.

Proper education opens the door to realization of the full potential of the individual, enabling a productive and fulfilling life, a net benefit to society—dharma. Failure in education leads to a life of stress, mistakes, drug abuse, criminal activity, a net liability for society—a-dharma. Proper education is truly the cornerstone of a healthy society.

The field of education has become a battleground over the goals and methods of education. This "debate" would be far more productive if it were focused on identifying the vocations and skill sets to enable each student to find their place in society in a way that is personally fulfilling and most beneficial to society—in other words, to find their dharma. It's more than a career—it's *dharma*!

The concept of dharma provides an overarching perspective that can guide policy considerations for optimal benefit to individuals, and a balanced society.

Notes

1. Maharishi Mahesh Yogi. 1969. *Bhagavad Gita: A New Translation and Commentary, Chapters 1-6*. Penguin. New York, N.Y. p 26.

9

Truth

> Whoever undertakes to set himself up as a judge of Truth and Knowledge is shipwrecked by the laughter of the gods.
> —*Albert Einstein*

Throughout history, various camps have attempted to impose their version of *the truth* on everyone else.

The gods may be laughing, but the rest of us pay a heavy price for this tendency to define and attempt to enforce "our truth" on other people.

It is entirely natural and healthy that on any given issue there will be a wide variety of perspectives and opinions. This variety in the body politic is like a healthy variegated ecosystem. When any one group attempts to impose its viewpoint on the whole by suppressing others, the natural vitality of the entire system is degraded, in the same way that mono-cropping degrades the soil.

It is a difficult test for many, and a sign of maturity, to be able to transcend superficial differences of opinion and embrace the broader, more unifying values and principles underlying those differences. A meeting ground, a commonality, can always be found if the intention and agreement is to work toward solutions, rather than allow gridlock born of intractable opposition.

If we wish to live a better life and leave a better world, we need to learn how to hold to our own truth, while allowing others theirs. We can radically improve our political process and our prospects going forward by embracing and promoting this mutual respect and tolerance as a bedrock cultural value, and expect and demand the same of our leaders.

10

Base or Fine

Be the change that you wish to see in the world.

—*Mahatma Gandhi*

The concepts of base and fine can be applied to almost any field of study or endeavor.

When applied to human affairs, base values[1] are "morally low, dishonorable, mean spirited, selfish, cowardly." Fine values[2] are the opposite of base: "morally superior, honorable, compassionate, generous, courageous."

Base values are degrading and cause suffering. Fine values are constructive and life supporting.

If polled on this matter, there would be few, if any, who would not state a preference to live in a world defined by fine values. Who wouldn't want to live in a peaceful, prosperous, compassionate and honorable world? But looking at the world we live in, it is apparent that we are not translating our common desire into experience through our actions.

Our government wages continuous war around the world. Those who speak out against war on principle are treated as threats to national security, and closely monitored by security services.

Our economy is structured to reward greed. With few exceptions, the biggest winners are those who extract maximum value while giving the minimum in return. Corporate managers are incentivized to exploit every opportunity for short term gain, and let the long term consequences fall where they may.

Our political process more closely resembles trench warfare than pursuit of the common good. Honest and respectful debate in pursuit of the greatest good is entirely absent from our political process.

Our primary media outlets relentlessly promote drama, conflict and scandal, and do little actual journalism.

But this world didn't happen all by itself. It didn't happen *to* us. We are all directly contributing to the creation and perpetuation of the world as it is. We are, at a minimum, complicit with our attention to and tolerance of all the above conditions, if not our active participation.

If we wish to change the world as we have created it, we have the power to do so. The process begins within. We *can* change our thinking, and *be* the change we would like to see in the world.

Notes

1. *Base*, Dictionary.com, http://dictionary.reference.com/browse/base (May 18,2016).
2. *Fine*, Dictionary.com, http://dictionary.reference.com/browse/fine (May 18,2016).

11

Political Process

Politics is the means by which we organize, structure and govern our society.

Political *process* is the way we go about those fundamental tasks. Process is informed by the cultural values in which it unfolds, and by the nature and actions of the people who are drawn to participate in the context of those cultural values. The people influence the culture, and the culture influences the people. It is a continuous process, and it can be a virtuous or villainous cycle depending on how we respond to the day to day and year to year needs, opportunities and challenges life presents. Knowledge in; knowledge out. Garbage in; garbage out.

The product of our process is the world we live in.

We cannot have good product without good process.

12

The Age of Spiritual Machines

In 1999 Ray Kurzweil published a book with the astonishing title, *The Age of Spiritual Machines.*[1] The title is preposterous on the face of it, but Kurzweil has a spectacular track record for predicting the trajectory of technology, and has invented a variety of widely used technological applications. *Inc.* magazine has called him "the rightful heir to Thomas Edison."[2] His opinion merits respectful consideration.

By tracing the development of computing power back in time, Kurzweil demonstrates that the geometric curve of increasing computing power, a phenomenon known as Moore's Law, has been unfolding for millennia, but until recently the pace of development was too slow to be noticed as a phenomenon unto itself.

He then projects this phenomenon into the future, tracing the technological developments to be enabled by the now exponential advances in computing power, bringing us inevitably to a phase transition labeled the *singularity*[3] (also the title of a subsequent book), when humans will merge with their technology, creating a new life form.

Kurzweil projects that by 2030 computers will exceed the computing capacity of the human brain and that "when the machines claim to be conscious, we'll believe them."[4] He expects that by integrating biology with technology, and eventually transcending biology entirely, humans will gain extraordinary powers and be able to extend life indefinitely.

Kurzweil believes that this relentless development of computing power is a natural phenomenon, guided by the *law of accelerating returns;*[5] that it has probably taken place many times on other planets; and that a successful transition is by no means certain.

Notes

1. Kurzweil, Ray. 1999. *The Age of Spiritual Machines.* New York, NY. Penguin
2. *About*, Transdendentman.com, http://transcendentman.com/about/ (May 18, 2016).
3. *Technological_singularity* , Wikipedia, https://en.wikipedia.org/wiki/Technological_singularity (May 18, 2016).
4. Kurzweil, Liner notes.
5. *The-law-of-accelerating-returns* , Kurzweilai.net, http://www.kurzweilai.net/the-law-of-accelerating-returns (May 18, 2016).

13

The Age of Spiritual Machines (2)

We are as gods, and HAVE to get good at it.
–Whole Earth Discipline

In *The Age of Spiritual Machines* Kurzweil devotes a good deal of space to analyzing the benefits as well as potential hazards of nanotechnology, in particular the self-replicating feature of molecular assemblers, or nanobots.

Nanobots are molecular scale machines capable of reorganizing the biological material in their environment to replicate themselves. The tiny machines have seemingly endless beneficial applications. Like all technology, they also have inherent hazards and potentially destructive applications in the hands of malefic parties.

The most extreme potential hazard from nanotech is referred to as "gray goo,"[1] a term coined by nanotech pioneer Eric Drexler, describing the planetary outcome of exponential nanobot replication—all biological material on Earth reduced to "gray goo."

Nanotech is not the only technology with the potential to cause serious damage to human civilization. Nuclear power is the most obvious, but bio-tech and geo-engineering are also capable. The list is growing, and the Defense Advanced Research Projects Agency (DARPA) is probably developing technologies no-one knows about yet.

And the Mother of All Technologies, artificial intelligence (AI), will soon enable the consolidation and cross-fertilization of all of the other technologies.

Our species is *ascending* technologically. We are gaining god-like powers of creation and destruction, yet we remain mired in a primitive political paradigm. Our technological ascension must be accompanied by a commensurate elevation in our politics to ensure that our growing power is utilized for the greater good, and not for destruction.

It is instructive that we have been unable to negotiate a global nuclear nonproliferation treaty despite the clear and present danger to all of humanity presented by the proliferation of nuclear weapons. The *Bulletin of the Atomic Scientists* recently stated...

> Unchecked climate change, global nuclear weapons modernizations, and outsized nuclear weapons arsenals pose extraordinary and undeniable threats to the continued existence of humanity, and world leaders have failed to act with the speed or on the scale required to protect citizens from potential

> catastrophe. These failures of political leadership endanger every person on Earth.[2]

Absent an upgrade in our politics to match our technological ascension, the hazards represented by the failures in nuclear proliferation will steadily increase, and the consequences become more inevitable. The need for our collective attention to this matter is urgent.

Notes

1. *Grey Goo*, Wikipedia, https://en.wikipedia.org/wiki/Grey_goo (May 17, 2016).
2. *Three Minutes and Counting*, Bulletin of the Atomic Scientists, http://thebulletin.org/three-minutes-and-counting7938 (May 17, 2016).

14

The Mother of Invention

> This is the first moment in the history of our planet when any species, by its own voluntary actions, has become a danger to itself—as well as to vast numbers of others.[1]
>
> —*Bill Joy*

The toxic mixture of our advancing technology in context of our primitive politics is a more fundamental and pervasive problem than any the human race has faced to date.

The hypnotic allure of advancing technology is the dominant economic force of our time. Technological expansion provides limitless creative challenges for our brightest minds, and the promise of virtually unimaginable benefits in every field of human endeavor. It also holds the promise of unparalleled wealth and power for those who can win the race to control it.

The challenge lies in our ability to manage ourselves; to

transcend our more primitive impulses and join together to create the social mechanisms, institutions and cultural foundations to ensure that our technology is used for the greater good, and not for destruction.

This is an existential challenge that cannot be left to self-interested parties or rigid ideologues. It must be met by a pragmatic and representative effort, fueled by general awareness of the stakes, and a determination for success framed by the intention to benefit everyone. This will require an elevation of our political process commensurate with the challenge.

Our politics has been based on the premise of binary choices—management OR labor, Capitalism OR Socialism, conservative OR liberal, this religion OR that religion. These choices are based on the false premise of either/or. This is a primitive model that divides us and leads to endless conflict. The truth of the matter is that we need both management AND labor, Capitalism AND Socialism, conservatives AND liberals. And we need the essence of ALL religions.

Our technology is enabling us to transcend the limitations of the physical world. If we step up to an honorable political *process*, technology can also enable us to transcend the limitations of this divisive political paradigm.

If we can engage the issues before us with integrity, pragmatism, and a genuine ethic of public service, our technology will enable us to model various solutions for any issue and determine likely outcomes. Once a path forward is chosen, our technology will allow us to follow and adjust policy in real time in response to *actual* outcome.

We need the best of both liberal and conservative ideas to achieve optimal, balanced policy—and we can have the best of both if we elevate our political *process.*

It is both our existential need and our great opportunity to give rise to an *ascendant* political paradigm that will *transcend* conflict, *solve* the problems we face, and *resolve* the issues that divide us. This is our opportunity for greatness.

Notes

1. Bill Joy, *Why the Future Doesn't Need Us*, Wired.com, http://www.wired.com/2000/04/joy-2/ (May 18, 2016).

15

Our Challenge

We are like fighter pilots who can no longer tolerate the g-forces generated by the latest high performance jet fighters. The geometrically expanding capabilities of our technology are racing ahead of our ability to manage them. Increasingly they can only be managed by design—*a priori*—which is in turn informed by the values and intentions of the designers.

Artificial Intelligence (AI) is the looming pinnacle of our technological ascendance, and the ultimate example of the problem we face.

> ...**it's likely to be either the best or worst thing ever to happen to humanity**, so there's huge value in getting it right. We should shift the goal of AI from creating pure undirected artificial intelligence to creating beneficial intelligence. It might take decades to figure out how to do this, so let's start researching this today rather than the night before the first

strong AI is switched on.[1]
—*Stephen Hawking*

Economically, the implementation of advancing technology has already vastly expanded the reach of management, spawning consolidation in every industry, reducing diversity and competition at every level, and concentrating wealth and power in fewer and fewer hands.

This concentration of economic power has in turn resulted in the wholesale corruption of our political process and government, as self-interested parties vie to control policy in order to enhance their advantage and avoid accountability for their actions.

In the interview quoted above, Hawking was asked about the issue of technological unemployment, with robots and AI replacing most humans at work. Hawking responded that if the resources produced by the machines are shared fairly equitably, most people will be able to live a somewhat more luxurious life. If not shared, most people would end up "miserably poor" while the owners of the machines consolidate wealth, and that presently, we are trending toward the latter outcome.

This is not news to those who have been paying attention; and it raises a fundamental question underlying the massive dislocations being spawned by our advancing technology: *What is the purpose of our technology?*

Is advanced technology for the purpose of enabling a neo-feudal concentration of wealth and power, or is it for the purpose of freeing humanity from the drudgery of physical tasks and limitations, and opening the door to the flowering of human potential?

Are the humans here to serve the machines and their owners, or are the machines here to serve the humans?

The answers to these questions seem obvious. We have the opportunity to create a better life and a better world for everyone. But in fact, we are headed in exactly the opposite direction.

We are approaching a time, in fact have already entered a time, when the old economic paradigm no longer serves. Binary Capitalism-Socialism is a relic. We need to summon the political will to create a hybrid model that transcends the destructive conflict between these models and draws on the best features of both Capitalism and Socialism; that honors the needs of capital, encourages innovation, and rewards risk takers, while directing the development and applications of advanced technology to safeguard and uplift all of humanity.

Technology is opening the door to a whole new world in medicine, management, materials science, and virtually every other field. Technology can also enable the creation of a new political and economic paradigm.

Notes

1. *Stephen Hawking AMA*, Wired.com, http://www.wired.com/brandlab/2015/10/stephen-hawkings-ama/ (May 18, 2016).

16

Ethics

There was a time when terms like *virtue* and *character* were a part of normal conversation, reflecting values considered paramount in public life. Even a brief reading of the writings of the framers of the U.S. Constitution reveals a public morality deeply concerned with the character of those in public life.

Policy makers receiving favors from vested interests was once called what it is—bribery. Being caught accepting bribes was cause for shame and resignation, if not jail time. Today it's called "campaign finance"; it's systemic, legal and *everyone does it.*

Even as recently as the 1970's, there was an expectation that those in public life should uphold high standards, and be held accountable if they faltered. In 1974 Richard Nixon became the only U.S. President to resign his office, as a result of fallout from the Watergate scandal, when Senators *from his own party* demanded he step down.

Today such events are treated as public relations issues. Those caught in shady dealings call in the spin doctors, mount a public relations campaign, attack the source of revelations, deny responsibility, apologize to the people, and go to a treatment center for a month or two. And thereafter, they insist that it's all "old news" and move on as if nothing had ever happened.

We need a better model for leadership and a public ethic that attracts and rewards those who genuinely want to serve the public interest, rather than the current model of non-accountability, which attracts people with base motives and incentivizes bad behavior.

It would be easy enough to reign in the epidemic of corrupt practices, if the people demanded it. Things would change quickly if every state and the federal government had robust, independent ethics commissions, with subpoena power and a mandate for aggressive, fast track action against corrupt officials.

When someone takes up a position of public trust, they need to know that they will be held to the highest standard, and that there will be swift and serious consequences for violating that trust.

And when someone has violated the public trust, restoration to a position in public life should not follow from a peremptory display of remorse. If such a person should *ever* be restored to a position of public trust, a genuine change of heart and mind demonstrated in action over a long period of time should be a minimal requirement.

This is ultimately a cultural matter, emanating from the people. As long as we tolerate corrupt practices, and give our support to those who engage in such practices, the status quo will continue.

17

The Arc of Policy

Policy should adjust for changing conditions and the need of the times. The same issue may at one point call for engaged action, and at another point, a laissez-faire approach.

A good example is the monetary model called Keynesian economics. John Maynard Keynes was a British economist who advocated government intervention to moderate the boom and bust extremes of the modern capitalist business cycle. His model acts as a damper at extremes, calling for fiscal and monetary stimulus to stimulate aggregate demand during times of recession, and withdrawing the stimulus during times of expansion.

Keynesian economics is the basis of the Federal Reserve's repeated campaigns since 2008, known as Quantitative Easing (QE) 1, 2 and 3, to stimulate the economy and save it from deflationary recession, otherwise known as economic collapse.

Keynesian economics has fallen into disrepute in some quarters because of the propensity for policy makers to inject stimulus during recessions, and to inject *more* stimulus during expansion instead of withdrawing it. This habit exacerbates the extremes instead of damping them, and runs up huge deficits in the process.

Beginning with the Long Term Capital Management episode[1] in 1998 the Federal Reserve has met each new (and worse) financial crisis with increased stimulus, while refusing to reign in the abuses causing the growing instability. This run-on stimulus has culminated in the sustained QE campaign from 2008 onward, and resulted in trillion dollar deficits, a debacle from which there does not appear to be any graceful exit.

A dispassionate examination of history in this matter suggests that the problems resulting from the application of Keynesian economics are not the result of Keynes' model, but from the unprincipled misapplication of the model by financial and political interests attempting to juice expansionary periods for the benefit of their narrow interests, while sacrificing the general welfare during the inevitable contraction phase in order to protect their gains.

These abuses inevitably lead to debasement of the currency. Keynes himself had this to say about the destructive consequences of debasing the currency:

> There is no subtler, no surer means of overturning the existing basis of society than to debauch the currency. The process

> engages all the hidden forces of economic law on the side of destruction, and does it in a manner which not one man in a million is able to diagnose.

This example highlights two principles:

1. Policy needs to adjust to changing conditions. Keynes' model is an excellent example and guide for the pragmatic and practical application of policy to promote the general welfare.
2. No policy, no matter how brilliant, can save us from the machinations of base leadership. If we want a better outcome, we need better leaders, who will value and apply wise, disciplined, and pragmatic policy in a spirit of public service.

Notes

1. *Case Study: Collapse of Long-Term Capital Management*, FinanceTrain.com, http://financetrain.com/case-study-collapse-of-long-term-capital-management/ (May 18, 2016).

18

The Wealth of a Nation

The distribution of wealth in human society has undoubtedly been a bone of contention for as long as there has been human society. Wealth brings power, and control of that wealth is the underlying driver of most of the distortions, corruption, conflict and violence in the world. It is often said that if you want to know the ultimate source of any man-made calamity, "follow the money."

It is beyond both the reach and object of policy to negate the primal impulse for wealth and power. However, there are things that can be done to channel these impulses into honorable and constructive activities, and to mitigate the imbalances created from excessive concentrations of wealth and power.

There is much talk these days about the disparity in wealth and income, with the top 1% having taken in virtually all of the economic gains generated since 2008, a period during which the vast majority has been losing ground.

Historically, the concentration of wealth in the upper tier is not an outlier. In fact, the roughly 50 year period following the end of WWII, the era of the great American middle class, was the real outlier.[1] This was a period of unprecedented gain for the masses, many of whom realized *the American Dream*—home ownership, education, family and upward mobility. The top tier did well also, but the economic pie was fairly equitably shared based on policy developments growing out of the Great Depression, and a public ethic of shared growth.

Beginning in 1980 the pendulum began to swing the other way with the election of Ronald Reagan and the ascendance of supply-side economics, also known as Reaganomics, trickle-down economics, or as George Bush Sr. famously called it, *voodoo economics.* Supply-side economics became the national economic religion.

Simply stated, the rationale of supply-side economics holds that lowering tax rates and reducing government regulation will create economic growth by increasing investment in businesses that *supply* goods and services, and the benefits from that growth will flow to the rest of society in the form of jobs and a greater supply of goods and services at lower prices. A thorough discussion of the theory is available here.[2]

The supply-side paradigm spawned repeated rounds of tax cuts and regulatory retreats. Proponents claimed the tax cuts would stimulate so much growth that tax revenues would actually increase. The actual result was massive increases in deficit spending and public debt, and the steady migration of wealth and income from the general public to the upper tier. Concurrently, the regulatory retreat enabled the epic scale fraud in the financial sector that yielded the economic crisis of 2008, and the ongoing recession to date.

The wealth of a nation is like the blood in a body. It needs to circulate everywhere in order to maintain optimal health. Excess concentration in any one area, whether public or private, leaves other areas underserved, creating imbalance and instability.

We have seen the catastrophic consequences of excessive control of wealth by the state. One only needs to look at the corruption and stagnation of Russia, Cuba, and Venezuela to see the results of this path. Free enterprise and self-determination have clearly demonstrated superiority for generating economic growth and social progress.

On the other hand, excessive concentration of wealth in the upper tier of the private sector also results in corruption, and misallocation of resources, creating asset bubbles and non-productive rent seeking.

Several recent studies[3] have demonstrated that wealthy individuals demonstrate a tendency to become increasingly self-absorbed and separate from society. This is not the beneficial effect of success and growing wealth one would hope for, for those individuals, or for society as a whole.

Ideally, our most successful and wealthy citizens would consider themselves invested in and part of society, rather than separate from and above it. This argues for consideration of policies and incentives to redirect the efforts of our most successful citizens from increasing isolation and narcissism, to engaged responsibility—a revival of the principle of *noblesse oblige.*

Notes

1. Piketty, Thomas. 2014. *Capital in the Twenty-First Century*. Cambridge, MA. Harvard University Press. pp 23-24
2. *Supply-side economics*, Wikipedia, https://en.wikipedia.org/wiki/Supply-side_economics (August 16, 2016).
3. *Wealthy Selfies: How Being Rich Increases Narcissism*, Time.com, http://healthland.time.com/2013/08/20/wealthy-selfies-how-being-rich-increases-narcissism/ (May 18, 2016).

19

The Flowering of Humanity

> Life is what we make it. Always has been; always will be.
> –*Grandma Moses*

We have long been told that humans use approximately 10% of their potential. We all have our own personal notions of what would constitute complete self-actualization. Our vision of possibilities is necessarily limited by our cultural milieu, and the constraints of our personal experience, but might include ideas such as transformational leader, Jedi warrior, or market, musical or numerical savant. For most of us, great wisdom, charisma, insight and empathy would be part of the package. Generally, these ideas are larger than life.

Living and expressing one's full potential need not be expressed or demonstrated through grand and visible accomplishments, and in most cases probably is not. Simple roles may also be the backdrop against which life is lived to its fullest potential.

In traditional terms, *enlightenment* is considered the pinnacle of human development. Individuals who have attained true and lasting enlightenment have left mankind insights into their state of being. Their teachings have inspired great religious and philosophical traditions.

This potential to be fully realized goes beyond individual realization; it extends to society as a whole.

The notion of a realized *society*, comprised of multitudes of realized citizens is something for which we have no benchmark. The multiplier effect of great numbers of individually realized citizens reinforcing each other would likely create an exalted human experience, and a world we would hardly recognize.

One thing is clear: the flowering of human potential on a broad scale would need to be nurtured in the context of supportive social and economic conditions. Our most underdeveloped natural resource is our human potential. If we want to maximize that resource, we will need to provide the conditions and resources to cultivate it just as we would, and do, for any other natural resource we want to develop.

20

The Spiritual Element of Life

In modern times the concept of "spiritual" has become synonymous with "the other side" of life, something vague, possibly mystical—not the worldly, practical, everyday part of life. It is something to turn to during brief periods of introspection, or a time of tragedy.

The compartmentalization of the spiritual element of life reflects the fragmentation and isolation of personal life in our hyper-materialistic society, while simultaneously informing our actions in the world, and the nature of our relations with each other.

This compartmentalized worldview overlooks the reality that the spiritual element of life is the *whole* of life. It is the universal, unifying value underlying and infusing all the "parts" in personal life, and connecting all humans with each other and their world in common.

Any comprehensive strategy for dealing with the areas of

common concern in human society would not be complete without consideration of the spiritual element of life.

Our world, and everything and everyone in it, all deserve the basic honor and respect due their status as an integral part of the whole of life. Failure to recognize this underlying reality leads to fragmentation, tribalism and endless conflict.

Politics in America today could not be further removed from wholeness. Base politicians and media engage the worst of our primitive impulses, deliberately promoting division, disrespect, conflict, fear and hatred of "the other." Disrespect and demonization of opposition have become hallmarks of our politics.

When we are busy demonizing our opponents, it would be unseemly to sit down with them to determine common cause. Demonstrations of "principled" opposition become more important than solutions. Compromise is seen as surrender.

As a result we see absurd and wasteful outcomes like the Republican controlled House of Representatives passing at least 60 bills[1] to undermine or repeal Obamacare—every one of them guaranteed to be vetoed by Obama—the most recent on Groundhog Day,[2] without ever making an actual effort to negotiate a better health care outcome for the American people.

How different our national life would be if the universal perspective of the wholeness of life were a lively backdrop to political process and policy considerations. It would provide a supportive foundation for mutual respect, honorable process, conflict resolution and the crafting of policy solutions meeting the needs of all parties, and society as a whole.

Notes

1. *House Sends Obamacare Repeal Bill to White House*, CNN.com, http://www.cnn.com/2016/01/06/politics/house-obamacare-repeal-planned-parenthood/ (August 20, 2016).
2. *GOP Lawmakers Vote to Repeal Obamacare, Again, On Groundhog Day*, ThinkProgress.org, https://thinkprogress.org/gop-lawmakers-vote-to-repeal-obamacare-again-on-groundhog-day-6f0c931a8549#.zby2t9tma (August 20, 2016)

21

Pragmatism

Satisfactory resolution of an issue is generally best served by determining what actually *works* to accomplish the desired end. This is the definition of the term *pragmatic.*

The objective of public policy is a resolution of a public need or desire with a positive outcome in the greatest common good, not a special interest carve out, nor an ideologically pure effort, regardless of outcome.

During the consideration of any issue, it is good practice and basic common sense to survey the range of possible alternatives, before settling on an *initial* course of action. First efforts are rarely perfect, so tracking, measuring and adjusting incrementally to improve results, while periodically reviewing assumptions in light of predicted outcomes, is also basic common sense and good practice. This chain of events is what we would naturally see in the context of an overarching ethic of public *service.*

It sounds simple. And it *could* be. The elements of principled debate and negotiation are well known and are addressed thoroughly in a large literature on the art and science of mediation. So why is it that a principled and balanced outcome to issues of public concern, or even an honest debate, so often seems to escape us as a society?

The influence of our media has become a major obstacle to effective policy formation. A pragmatic outcome in service to the greatest common good is simply not achievable in a fact-free environment where the daily news cycle is committed to hyping fear-provoking events and directing public attention to the latest conspiracy theory, sex scandal or manufactured controversy.

From 1949 to 1987 the Fairness Doctrine[1] served as a structural support for balance in public discourse, requiring broadcasters to present contrasting viewpoints on issues of public concern, and do so in an honest, equitable and balanced manner. It was not a panacea for partisan excess, but it reflected a general expectation of honorable standards in the debate over public policy issues, and was reflected in a functional bipartisan willingness to compromise.

Since the demise of the Fairness Doctrine in 1987, our public discourse has become a "free-fire" (and often fact-free) zone, where partisans of all stripes can promote conspiracy theories, make up "facts" to suit their agenda—even deny demonstrable reality—and still be featured as credible by our media. This has resulted in a collapse of standards for honesty and integrity in public life, which has increasingly become dominated by those who will say or do anything to gain attention and/or advantage.

A circus-like media environment featuring headlines reminiscent of carnival barkers and one-sided, conflict-provoking coverage of political issues and events have become the norm, feeding a trend of polarization that has reached levels not seen since the Civil War.[2]

The result has been a schism in national consciousness and competing, incompatible narratives on all matters in the public sphere, making it impossible to find resolution on any of an ever growing list of critical issues.

It is not too much to ask to have honest, informative debate on the issues and decide collectively on our course of action. Nor is it too much to expect follow-up to that initial decision with a structured, unbiased method of measuring and reporting outcome over time, so adjustments can be made as needed.

Notes

1. *Fairness_Doctrine*, Wikipedia, https://en.wikipedia.org/wiki/Fairness_Doctrine (May 18, 2016).
2. *It's Been 150 Years Since the U.S. Was This Politically Polarized*, Gizmodo.com, http://io9.gizmodo.com/its-been-150-years-since-the-u-s-was-this-politically-1590076355 (June 8, 2016).

22

Paradox

> The truest sayings are paradoxical.
> —*Sun Tzu*

One quality of the wise is the ability to embrace paradox. A paradox is a statement or situation that is inherently conflicted, such as two opposing values or statements, each of which appears to be true on its own merits, but which cannot be true if the other is true.

Zeno, a Greek philosopher, advanced a number of famous paradoxes designed to demonstrate that motion is an illusion. Summed up, if an object is to travel from point A to point B, the object must first travel to the half way point between point A and point B. And in order to get to the half way point, it must first travel half way to that point, and so on into an infinity of half way points, demonstrating that migration from point A to point B cannot happen. Therefore, motion is not possible. Yet our senses tell us that motion does occur and that objects do indeed get somehow from point A to point B.

For those so inclined, Wikipedia has an excellent summary of Zeno's paradoxes,[1] and links to a variety of proposed solutions, from Aristotle to modern times.

The value of paradoxes is that they require thorough investigation into the nature of a phenomenon, promoting a deeper understanding than is gained from the acceptance of things as they first appear to be. The ability to embrace paradox enables the seeker to find the truth underlying contradictions. It requires an open-minded and unbiased commitment to conflict resolution, a valuable trait in any individual, and indispensable in those entrusted to formulate policy for society.

Notes

1. *Zeno's_paradoxes*, Wikipedia, https://en.wikipedia.org/wiki/Zeno's_paradoxes (May 18, 2016).

23

The Tradition of War

War is the continuation of politics by other means.
—*Carl von Clausewitz*

During the Vietnam War, returning soldiers were rejected and abused, called murderers and spat on in public places. Today the pendulum has swung 180 degrees and soldiers returning from Iraq and Afghanistan are universally greeted with "thank you for your service" and hailed as heroes.

Both of these responses are reactions of people who for the most part know nothing of the reality of war: the devastation, degradation, depravity and despair spawned by war. War, modern high intensity warfare in particular, subjects humans to experiences to which no one should ever be subjected. These experiences can dismantle the foundations of personality, and we have a very large number of veterans who are suffering from long-term invisible wounds.

Dealing honestly with the reality and consequences of war is a very delicate matter. Those who directly participate are reluctant to talk about it, and can have very intense emotional reactions to those who attempt to pry. Those with no direct experience are often quick to make judgments and express opinions.

The inner chaos and silent wounds created by direct involvement in war has long been ignored, seen as politically incorrect, and tactically inconvenient for the military, which relies on images and narratives of glory and heroism to recruit new generations of soldiers. In recent years, as our constant war fighting has steadily increased the number of walking wounded among us, the issue has demanded increased attention.

Post Traumatic Stress Disorder (PTSD) is the contemporary diagnosis, known in previous generations as "battle fatigue" or "shellshock," spawning an entire industry devoted to treating this malady. It has been a big step forward, finally acknowledging in a formal way the inner wounds sustained in combat. Yet we continue to lose more soldiers to suicide than we do to enemy action. In the U.S., veterans make up 7% of our population and over 20% of the suicides.[1] In my opinion this is because we have, to date, not been willing to deal with the elephant in the room—the moral issues inherent in warfare.

William P. Nash, a retired Navy psychiatrist who deployed in Fallujah in 2004 put it this way…

> I would bet anything, that if we had the wherewithal to do this kind of research we'd find that moral injury underlies veteran homelessness, criminal behavior, suicide.[2]

Rita Nakashima Brock and Gabriella Lettina authored a recent title, "Soul Repair: Recovering from Moral Injury after War."[3] *The Huffington Post* has sponsored an in-depth series on the internal consequences and *moral injuries* of war, the first in the series entitled "The Grunts: Damned if They Kill; Damned if They Don't,"[4] and *National Public Radio* did a piece on this topic, available here.[5]

As a society we do not adequately take responsibility for consequences to the individuals we send to war. These recent conversations and publications on moral injuries are a great step in the right direction.

Notes

1. Military Suicide Research Consortium, https://msrc.fsu.edu/news/media-misleads-military-veterans-suicide-study (May 18, 2016).
2. David Woods, *The Grunts: Damned if They Kill, Damned if They Don't*, Huffington Post, http://projects.huffingtonpost.com/moral-injury/the-grunts (May 18, 2016).
3. Brock, Rita Nakashima and Gabriella Lettini. 2012. *Soul Repair: Recovering From Moral Injury after War*. Boston, MA. Beacon Press.
4. Woods
5. *Moral Injury: The Psychological Wounds of War*, NPR.org,

http://www.npr.org/2012/11/21/165663154/moral-injury-the-psychological-wounds-of-war (May 18, 2016).

24

The Tradition of War (2)

> War is essentially an evil thing: its consequences are not confined to the belligerent states alone, but affect the whole world. To initiate a war of aggression therefore is not only an international crime, it is the supreme international crime, differing from the other war crimes in that it contains within itself the accumulated evil of the whole.[1]
>
> —*Robert H. Jackson*, U.S. Supreme Court Justice and Chief American Prosecutor at The International Military Tribunal at Nuremberg, 1946

There is responsive or defensive war, engaged in by those who are attacked by aggressors, or who come to the aid of the attacked, and there is aggressive war, that which was addressed by Robert H. Jackson at the Nuremberg Tribunal.

The former is a duty of every citizen. The latter is a violation of every known human and natural law. The state sanctioned slaughter of other human beings to attain political objectives is an abomination. Those who organize and promote such activities are criminals, and nations that allow themselves to be governed by such criminals pay a dear price in the end, and rightly so.

We like to think of ourselves as *civilized*, sophisticated and advanced beyond primitive cultures. But our sophistication is merely a thin veneer. Instead of ritual warfare and hand to hand combat, we wage high intensity war with advanced technology, with the greatest powers among us threatening annihilation by nuclear holocaust.

It doesn't take much analysis of this issue to see how unproductive and limiting it is for humanity, and what a horrible waste of resources and human potential. The tradition of war is a vestige of primitive culture we need to abandon if we wish to survive the massive increase in destructive power enabled by our advanced technology.

Notes

1. *Nuremburg Trials Proceedings Volume 22*, The Avalon Project, http://avalon.law.yale.edu/imt/09-30-46.asp (May 18, 2016).

25

Fear

The only thing we have to fear is fear itself.[1]
—*Franklin Roosevelt*

The emotion of fear is rooted in the most primitive part of the human brain, governing issues related to survival. Fear is an essential autonomic function in response to genuine threats to survival, such as "train coming" when we're standing on the tracks, or the sight of a man brandishing a gun in a shopping mall. In the modern world, however, many of the fears we have are not in response to genuine threats, but self-generated, stress related, and often promoted by external parties.

It is fear itself that is the real threat in our society. The constant stimulation of the fear response ("fight or flight") has a degrading effect on individual mental and physical health[2] and a coarsening effect on our society.[3]

Modern political operators, marketers and media have become skilled at provoking a fear response to attract followers for their specific agendas. The current media-generated hysteria over "terrorists" is a case study of the phenomenon.

Yes, misguided people with murderous intent ("terrorists") do exist, but they are few, and certainly not an existential threat to America. In fact, the odds of any American being killed by a terrorist are something on the order of 1 in 20 million.[4] Any individual American is 35,000 times more likely to die from heart disease than from terrorist action; 6,000 times more likely to die from medical error; 110 times more likely from contaminated food; 22 times more likely from a brain eating amoeba, and far more likely to become President or date a supermodel, than die from terrorist action.[5] The contagion of hysteria over "terrorists" is a mass media event, promoted by base politicians, war profiteers and their hired hands.

The campaign is having its effect. In early 2016, apparently having learned nothing from the catastrophic invasion of Iraq and the chaos that has engulfed the Middle East as a result of that invasion, a large percentage of the American people appeared willing to give their support to political candidates anxious to take us to war again in the Middle East.

If there is something to be feared, it is these candidates.

Fear, like vengeance, makes horrible policy; it is profoundly destructive and degrading to both individual life and society. To the extent that we give our attention and support to those individuals and groups seeking to manipulate us into supporting their agendas by provoking fear, we pay the price for that support.

The full measure of human potential cannot be realized in the context of pervasive, metastasizing fear. We would do well to heed Roosevelt's advice, and seek to elevate to leadership individuals with a demonstrated ability to evaluate threats, both real and imagined, with cool reason rather than primal fear, and who will act to limit the ability of mass media to hype negative events and generate hysteria for the sake of profits.

Notes

1. *FDR's First Inaugural Address*, History Matters: The U.S. Survey Course on the Web, http://historymatters.gmu.edu/d/5057/ (May 18, 2016).
2. *Chronic Stress Puts Your Health at Risk*, MayoClinic.org, http://www.mayoclinic.org/healthy-lifestyle/stress-management/in-depth/stress/art-20046037 (May 18, 2016).
3. *Social Consequences of Stress*, CoachingPositivePerformance.com, http://www.coachingpositiveperformance.com/social-consequences-of-stress/ (May 18, 2016).
4. Zeeshan ul Hassan, *A Data Scientist Explains Odds of Dying in a Terrorist Attack*, Techjuice.pk, http://www.techjuice.pk/a-data-scientist-explains-odds-of-dying-in-a-terrorist-attack/ (May 18, 2016).
5. *The Terrorism Statistics Every American Needs to Hear*, GlobalResearch.org, http://www.globalresearch.ca/the-terrorism-statistics-every-american-needs-to-hear/5382818 (May 18, 2016).

26

Truth (2)

> Never be afraid to raise your voice for honesty and truth and compassion against injustice and lying and greed. If people all over the world...would do this, it would change the earth.
> –William Faulkner

In the context of the normal interactions and discourse of life, truth is about honesty and personal integrity. We may see things differently, but we can present our views honestly and discuss our differences with integrity. And we can hold honesty and integrity as central cultural values and demand these qualities of our leaders.

Few would argue with the contention that the casual disregard of truth is a hallmark of public discourse today. I would go further and say that we live in a culture of deceit. Spin is *in* and cleverness is in vogue. An honest man or woman in public life today is viewed as a "boy scout" or "girl scout," derided by the power players.

The state of public debate today is such that it has become virtually impossible for the general public to gain an understanding of the issues and make informed decisions.

It stands to reason that when disinformation is the order of the day from our "leaders" and news media, the information needed for assessment and decisions by the public will be lacking, and important matters will go unresolved. If they *are* resolved, it will most likely be to the detriment of the general welfare.

27

On Unity

Unity is the underlying reality of life. The more we expand our frame of reference, the more clearly we perceive the interconnectedness of all life. This perception has profound implications for how relate to each other, and how we conduct our affairs, individually and collectively.

Through the lens of unity, the understanding dawns that we are *one tribe* here on planet Earth, intimately connected to each other and to the world around us. Ultimately our ability to survive will be dependent on our ability to recognize and organize around that reality.

The underlying unity of life expresses itself in the field of opposites: yin and yang, plus and minus, male and female. When in a balanced state, these opposites co-exist in a natural, dynamic and mutually supportive opposition to each other, creating a unified and harmonious whole greater than the sum of the parts. *Balance* is the central principle of natural law, operating constantly and pervasively to maintain the stability and integrity of the opposing values, and of their relationship to the multitude of expressed values of life.

The underlying unity of life is eternal and constant; the diverse, individual expressions of life are limited and ever-changing.

When any limited expression of life wanders off the reservation, or ignores the natural limitations of its status and context, it creates imbalance in the whole. The force of natural law will inevitably respond with corrective action to restore balance. That correction will be commensurate with the degree of imbalance. *Human civilization is not exempt.*

Opposing forces are in dynamic relationship to each other. Every action or movement by one force creates a response from its opposite, and from countless others, to restore and maintain the balance and unity of the whole.

This responsive action to restore and maintain balance is inherent in the nature of our world. A fundamental question at the outset of any action, campaign or policy consideration should be: will this action or policy promote balance or redress an existing imbalance; or will it create excess, or lack, and therefore imbalance?

28

The Love Principle

> I believe that unarmed truth and unconditional love will have the final word in reality. That is why right, temporarily defeated, is stronger than evil triumphant.
> –Martin Luther King, Jr.

Love is the binding force. It connects and draws together; it enables and promotes unity. Love is the recognition of unity, of self, across the chasm of diversity and superficial isolation. Love is soft, but it endures and in the end it is the most powerful force in creation. Without love the human experiment on planet Earth would have been over long ago.

In the seemingly endless conflict and confusion of the low road in human affairs, a moment of love, of recognition and *contact* between humans, is like a sparkle of light shining through a keyhole into a dark and turbulent room. The door is there for us to open if we choose. We do not have to live in eternal conflict.

It is probably a novel idea for most, but the love principle has long been a fundamental driver in many public policy considerations, although not usually thought of in those terms. A wise leader will consider not just what he or she thinks or wants, but what others want or need as well as what is in the best interest of all.

The force of love is the underlying impetus in efforts to lend a helping hand to the least fortunate among us, and in efforts to sustain the health and vitality of our environment. It is also the fundamental principle behind efforts to maintain fiscal responsibility and the integrity of our currency. It is the driver of efforts to expand our limits and explore new experiences, as well as efforts to maintain stability and avoid unnecessary suffering resulting from excess.

The love principle is the driving force behind efforts of all kinds, from various philosophical perspectives, to maintaining balance, peace, prosperity and opportunity for all of us. These conditions are the precursors to, and the platform of support for, the full flowering of human potential.

Most of us recognize our interdependence when we face the world in context of our immediate family. Some of us see things that way in context of our church, or school, or business or other community. Some see our interdependence in context of their nation. And there are a relatively small number of people who see themselves as part of the human race—the whole of the human race. In order to survive the challenges ahead, and ultimately manifest the full potential of human civilization, we need to move a lot more people into the latter category.

Our collective capacity for resolving the challenges of life is virtually infinite. But we tend to squander our opportunities and resources in small mindedness and endless squabbling—even violence—over relatively small matters.

It is both our challenge and opportunity to step up to a higher mode of civilization by consciously and deliberately incorporating the love principle in our political process and public policy formation.

29

The Politician's Dilemma

A recent *New Yorker* cartoon pictured a politician addressing his staff. The caption reads:

> Have you figured out how I can be on the right side of history without being on the wrong side of now?

This is the politician's dilemma.

The public servant who attempts to do that which serves the greater good will often find him or herself in opposition to single issue ideologues, or to vested interests that may not receive the protection, the tax break, the regulatory relief or regulatory imposition on their competition that they desire. In our no-holds-barred political environment, those disappointed special interests will be likely to finance slanderous attack ads in order to undermine the politician who doesn't play ball, in order to elect an opponent who will be more amenable to their interests. When faced with the choice of favoring the greater good, or getting re-elected, it is the rare politician who chooses the former.

Crafting public policy that addresses the need of the times; serves the greater good; takes into consideration all of the disparate needs and desires of the many constituencies affected, and considers the downstream effects of policy, is a sublime and consuming process. Doing it well takes a lot of time and focus.

Our politicians don't have time for that. They operate in a system that requires huge financial expenditures to guarantee re-election, and demands their time and attention to raise those funds. In 2012 the average House winner spent $1.5 million; the average Senate winner over $10 million.[1] Within the context of this system, our representatives need to spend most of their time fundraising, and subsequently tending to the needs of their financiers.

The above-described system is the portrait of a culture of corruption. In Washington, if one wants peer acceptance, and to get re-elected, one needs to adapt to that culture. Those who manage to get into office and are disinclined to adapt are marginalized, and usually don't stay long.

Politicians are often heard lamenting the demands and the stress of fundraising. What they fail to note, however, is that they are in control of the system requiring them to do this fundraising, and have the power to change it.

Current office holders could end this toxic campaign finance system tomorrow, along with all the rest of the corrupt practices in Washington. But they don't end these practices, because despite the pressure and the stress of fundraising, and the unseemly arrangements with lobbyists and financiers, the system as it stands represents an almost insurmountable barrier for any challenger. Once "in," the office holder is hard to unseat. As long as they operate within the current system, the odds of re-election are 9-1 in favor of the incumbent.

Notes

1. Russ Choma, *Election 2012: The Big Picture Shows Record Cost of Winning a Seat in Congress*, OpenSecrets.org, https://www.opensecrets.org/news/2013/06/2012-overview.html (May 18, 2016).

30

Balance (2)

Dwight Eisenhower demonstrated what a real leader sounds like.

> "Each proposal must be weighed in light of a broader consideration; the need to maintain balance in and among national programs – balance between the private and the public economy, balance between the cost and hoped for advantages – balance between the clearly necessary and the comfortably desirable; balance between our essential requirements as a nation and the duties imposed by the nation upon the individual; balance between the actions of the moment and the national welfare of the future. Good judgment seeks balance and progress; lack of it eventually finds imbalance and frustration."

From the farewell address[1] of Dwight D. Eisenhower. January 17, 1961.

Notes

1. http://mcadams.posc.mu.edu/ike.htm

31

The Government That Governs Best

The more corrupt the state, the more numerous the laws.

—*Tacitus*

That government is best which governs least, because its people discipline themselves.

—*Thomas Jefferson*

Over 200 years ago Thomas Jefferson identified the key to optimal government. A strong nation is made up of strong, independent, self-reliant citizens.

"Minimal government footprint" means maximum freedom of self-determination for citizens. With freedom of self-determination comes responsibility. Each citizen is responsible to self-govern. This is true democracy, and the highest form of government.

This does not mean that formal government has no value, a misguided notion that has gained favor in some circles.

While self-governance is the best kind of governance, there are some things that individuals cannot accomplish individually, which must therefore be done collectively. Defense of the nation, public safety, dispute resolution, and preservation of the commonwealth are among them.

There are also things at which government excels, to the benefit of the whole of society. For example, basic research, which requires a long term commitment with no certainty of commercial application or reward. Private enterprise generally cannot afford to do this kind of research, but it benefits all of us. The development of the Internet, GPS and Magnetic Resonance Imaging are several current examples.

There are also things which require a common agreement, or rules of the road, in order to function in a complex society: transportation, the free flow of commerce and food safety, for example. Government is generally the mechanism through which we make and implement these agreements.

The basic concept allowing for the optimal expression of all of these functions is the principle of *freedom to* and *freedom from*. *Freedom to* choose one's own path in life and make the most of it, and *freedom from* imposition or damage from others pursuing their own interests.

In an optimal society, every individual and group within that society, while pursuing their own interests, disciplines themselves, governs themselves, takes responsibility for themselves, and conducts themselves honorably and respectfully within the context of the whole of society.

There will never be perfection in these matters, but if

these higher values become cultural bedrock there will be little need, or demand, for the heavy hand of government to impose discipline. Every citizen and every sector will be oriented to self-discipline, and reign in their own excesses.

32

Corporatism

One of the primary polarizing and confusing influences in public life has been persistent, well financed lobbying and public relations campaigns backed by corporate interests. The efforts of these campaigns are always one sided, often to the point of deliberate misinformation, and tailored to the narrow interests of their patrons, not to the general welfare.

Every industry has its trade groups and political action committees (PAC's) promoting their interests by channeling money to lobbyists and candidates. Since every possible issue of general concern also impacts some corporate interest or another, there are virtually *no* issues that don't receive the attention of these groups. And when a big issue such as health reform arises, the money flow is downright astonishing.

A Center for Public Integrity analysis[1] of Senate lobbying disclosure forms for 2009 shows that more than 1,750 companies and organizations hired about 4,525 lobbyists—eight for each member of Congress—to influence health reform bills. And those are just the *declared* lobbyists.

Health care is something every citizen needs at some point in their life. It is an important and fundamentally non-partisan issue. However, due to the relentless distortion of this issue by corporate interests vested in the status quo, we may never have an honest debate on health care.

Environmental conservation is another issue of general concern that transcends left/right politics, and one that is *inherently* conservative. However, it is otherwise conservative interests that routinely oppose virtually all efforts to craft sound environmental policy.

The environment is our commonwealth. We are all dependent on it for life, and when it is violated we are all damaged. There is no natural polarity on this issue. But there are powerful corporate interests making billions of dollars by polluting the environment. If they were forced to clean up after themselves (i.e. assume the full cost of production), it would cost them a good deal of their profits. Not surprisingly they don't want to pay to clean up after themselves. They have been getting away with polluting the commonwealth and offloading the cost of cleanup onto the public for a long time, and they don't want to change.

The public relations campaigns employed in these matters are often framed in left/right political terms, utilizing subterfuge and inflammatory rhetoric to sow division and mistrust. They promote ideas that create confusion and often convince people to actually vote against their own interests, while casting fellow citizens with opposing views as the enemy.

These kinds of campaigns are morally bankrupt, and have had a profoundly destructive effect on the fabric of society.

The truth of the matter is that fundamental liberal and conservative concerns are like the left and right legs of the body politic. They are both needed to move forward. The notion that they are incompatible is a false notion promoted by people and organizations who hope to benefit their narrow interests by creating division and mistrust.

If we are to bootstrap ourselves up from the low road of our degraded political process, we must collectively agree to put a stop to these deliberately divisive, corrupting and profoundly dishonest practices.

Notes

1. Joe Eaton, *Lobbyists Swarm Capitol to Influence Health Reform*, The Center for Public Integrity, http://www.publicintegrity.org/2010/02/24/2725/lobbyists-swarm-capitol-influence-health-reform (May 18, 2016).

33

Pervasive Dishonesty

> Oh, what tangled web we weave, when first we practice to deceive.
>
> *–Sir Walter Scott*

Our public life has been eaten away by dishonesty, like termites in the floor joists. We have become so accustomed to the daily spin from partisans left and right, that we no longer expect anyone in public life to speak honestly, and don't believe it when they do.

As a result, we simply cannot have an informed discussion about anything, which precludes actually solving any problem or implementing any policy for the greater good. Partisan warfare has become so entrenched that it goes beyond trying to put a shine on your own position, or casting doubt on the opposition. It is now about preventing the opposition from gaining traction or having success on any front. The result is systemic failure—gridlock, that *trickles down* from the top, infecting the entire body politic.

Americans like to use their leaders as piñatas, but at the same time look up to them, and emulate them. Young people take their cues in their developmental years from the adults in their immediate world, and also from the leaders of society.

If our leaders demonstrate to our young people that those who get ahead, who rise to the top, are people who will say or do anything to gain advantage; who deny responsibility for any problems they have created; and who clearly have zero concern for the truth in any matter, then we are raising new generations which will emulate what they have been taught.

Is this the society we want?

Young people are acutely aware of both truthfulness and hypocrisy. They know they are being asked to ingest and abide by a system of lies and misinformation. Many of them reject this pressure and attempt to walk a more honorable path. With encouragement and support, *those* young people could just as easily become the next generation of leaders implementing the high road in politics.

34

Our Legacy

> While I thought that I was learning how to live, I have been learning how to die.
>
> —*Leonardo da Vinci*

We are all here in this world for a short time. Notwithstanding professions of great certainty on this matter, the fact that we are here at all is a great mystery, and one day each of us will leave. Where we have come from and to where we go after, if anywhere, are also great mysteries, in regard to which we turn to systems of *belief* we call religions.

In any case we have no control over the great mysteries of life. They simply *are*, and we have to deal with them as best we can, individually and collectively. What we *do* have control over is what we do while we are here—how we live our lives, and the legacy we leave for those who come after us.

The current generation can take pride in a number of accomplishments: a major extension of human lifespan, general improvement in quality of life globally, massive technological development enabling widespread access to education and skills training, huge improvements in medical technology, and the fact that humans globally are less likely to die a violent death today than at any time in history.

At the same time we engage in endless wars, continue to develop potentially civilization destroying weapons, and threaten the balance of nature and ultimately our own survival with environmental degradation. We allow the economic fruit of our technological ascendance to aggregate to a relative handful of families, creating great concentrations of wealth side by side with grinding poverty, and we accept widespread misbehavior at the highest levels of society.

We have allowed the fraud of "supply side economics" to virtually extinguish the American Dream in a single generation. Young people today are the first in American history to believe that they will not live a better quality of life than their parents.[1]

We can do better. When the time comes to account for my life, I for one would like to do so content that I have made a positive contribution to my heirs and have in some fashion left the world a better place. I imagine the vast majority of people would feel the same way if they took the time to think about it.

Our technological ascendance is giving us the power to fashion the world of our choosing. We have the means and the opportunity to set the stage for the unfoldment of human potential as never before, and enable the flowering of humanity into a fully realized civilization.

Carpe diem!

Notes

1. Elizabeth Mendez, *In U.S., Optimism About Future for Youth Reaches All-Time Low*, Gallup.com, http://www.gallup.com/poll/147350/optimism-future-youth-reaches-time-low.aspx (May 18, 2016).

PART 2

Process: Getting From Here to There

The first action required to upgrade our political process is to remove the obstacles to the upgrade.

35

Setting the Stage

> The unleashed power of the atom has changed everything save our modes of thinking...We shall require a substantially new manner of thinking if mankind is to survive.
>
> —*Albert Einstein*

Technology is delivering to us the means to decide on the future we will create. The outcome is dependent on how we organize ourselves and how we deal with each other—our politics.

The elements of healthy, balanced, honorable political process apply to every level of human interaction, from personal relationships to geopolitics. In this book the focus is on the macro level of national politics, because that is the level affecting the most people, and our society as a whole.

Ultimately, people get the government they deserve. If our political process is degraded it is because we have allowed it to become degraded. We have to step up our game if we want better leadership, better policy, and a more just and sustainable society. If we fail to step up, the future will be arranged for us, either by despots or by nature, or both.

Core elements of an upgraded political process are recognition of our common humanity and interdependence, recognition of the value of opposing viewpoints and reality-based debate, cultivation of the habit of transcending conflict to seek solutions, and elevation of wise and mature citizens to leadership.

Currently, the way *upward* is obstructed by an interlocking matrix of toxic influences; campaign finance, private lobbying, corrupt political parties and divisive media, all fueled by the flow of money from vested corporate interests and enabled by a complacent citizenry.

These influences must be neutralized before we can heal our political process and begin to deal with the growing list of urgent public policy issues, the greatest of which is the management of the exponentially expanding power of our technology.

In order to restore balance and set the stage for the elevation of public life, we will first need to…

1. Take responsibility
2. Set a higher standard
3. Get the money out of politics
4. Reject the demagogues
5. Govern the corporations

6. Limit the concentration of power
7. Hold officials accountable
8. Separate news and entertainment
9. Withdraw from empire
10. Attend to the (political) process

As a collection of individual problems, the task of restoring balance seems impossible. Each area listed above has many deep pocket vested interests that will bury any efforts at incremental reform under a blizzard of lawsuits, delays, distractions, misinformation, character assassination, etc.

However, the imbalances in each of these areas are the symptoms of a *fundamental* imbalance at the foundation of our society. This fundamental imbalance is a reflection of the *collective consciousness* of the nation. Healing the imbalances in each area will require simultaneous efforts to heal the fragmentation and polarization of the collective consciousness of the nation.

The *only* model I am aware of to support and heal imbalances in society on the level of collective consciousness, the whole of society, was initiated by Maharishi Mahesh Yogi, with his *coherence-creating groups*, comprised of large numbers of people practicing Transcendental Meditation together.

The principle behind the coherence-creating groups is that collective consciousness is a field, subject to field effects. Every individual both contributes to and is affected by the entire field of collective consciousness.

If a majority of individuals in society is conflict-oriented, then society will be conflict-oriented. If the majority is stressed, society will be stressful. Conversely, if a majority of individuals is oriented to transcend conflict and find common cause with their neighbors, then society will be peaceful. If a majority of individuals is self-realized, then society will be self-actualizing.

Presently, our society is stressed, imbalanced, divided and conflict-oriented. As the pain consequent to the rise of imbalance and stress in our society becomes intolerable, people are beginning to wake up and demand change. The first lesson on the path to the high road is to realize that change begins within.

Society is a reflection of the aggregate contributions of all the members of society—the collective consciousness of all the people. Coherence-creating groups can enhance the quality of collective consciousness by aggregating and amplifying the beneficial effects [1] of Transcendental Meditation for the practicing individuals. This effect has been the focus of numerous scientific studies, and has been called the Maharishi Effect.[2]

The rise of populist movements in the 2016 Presidential campaign led by Socialist Bernie Sanders on the left, and Fascist-leaning Donald Trump on the right, are a clear sign that people are waking up. The question we now face is whether the nascent awakening of 2016 will be channeled into another round of conflict, as it has thus far, perpetuating the downward spiral of public life, or whether the vision will expand to perceive the need to transcend conflict and come together as a nation to resolve our differences.

When a critical mass of people embraces the wisdom of the need to transcend differences to solve problems, balance will be restored rapidly, and our society will begin to be transformed into a self-actualizing civilization.

Notes

1. *What's the evidence?* TM.org, http://www.tm.org/research-on-meditation (September 30, 2016).
2. *Modern Science Documents the Maharishi Effect*, GlobalGoodNews.com, http://maharishi-programmes.globalgoodnews.com/maharishi-effect/research.html (September 17, 2016).

36

Take Responsibility

> The world is a dangerous place, not because of the people who do evil things; but because of those who do nothing about it.
> —*Albert Einstein*

A republic is a form of social organization in which the power of society rests ultimately with the citizens, who elect their representatives at government. These representatives are in turn held accountable to the people and to the rule of law, theoretically at least.

I doubt most people feel that our representatives are held accountable to the law. And the reason that our representatives are not held accountable to the law is because we don't *hold* them accountable. We don't demand it. In fact, one of the perquisites of power in 21st Century America is that, with rare exceptions, you are explicitly *not* held accountable to the law.

The condition of our society; the partisan warfare, the economic dislocations, the unjust and unequal application of the law, the rampant corruption and dishonesty in public life, are all *our* creation—we the people. If dishonorable people have seized the reins of power and do evil things with that power, it is because we have allowed them to do so.

We can say we want a more responsible society and integrity in public life, but if we think someone *else* is responsible for current conditions, we are assuming a victim position, a position of weakness, from which it will be difficult, if not impossible, to make constructive changes in the status quo.

If, however, we decide to accept responsibility for the current condition of public life, even if it's not readily apparent how we have created it, then we are assuming a position of strength, and the results of our efforts will reflect that strength.

Change begins within. These principles apply both individually and collectively.

37

Set a Higher Standard

> True fellowship among men must be based upon a concern that is universal. It is not the private interests of the individual that create lasting fellowship among men, but rather the goals of humanity.
> –I Ching

Few would argue against the statement that our standards for honesty in public discourse and honor in public service have become very low. We have come to expect blatant dishonesty from our public servants. And with rare exceptions, there is no penalty for betraying the public interest in favor of personal or partisan interests.

The methods for gaining re-election have become so refined, and the public response so predictable, that with adequate financial backing re-election is virtually guaranteed. In 2014 96% of incumbents seeking re-election were re-elected despite public approval of Congress at 11%.[1] In 2012 the incumbent re-election rate was 90% while approval of Congress hit an all-time low of 10%.[2] We complain in disapproval, but it seems we are getting precisely the government we are asking for at the polls.

The disconnect between our rational disapproval of our representatives in government, and irrational support for them at election time is self-destructive, effectively leaving the public sphere to self-interested parties who have become entitled to do whatever they please, regardless of any harm to the nation or to humanity.

We are allowing our reason and self-interest to be overshadowed by moral and genetic triggers activated by sophisticated and insidious public relations tactics. Jonathan Haidt has detailed the primal impulses dividing us and the triggers being utilized to exacerbate divisions and manipulate our behavior in his brilliant work, *The Righteous Mind: Why Good People Are Divided by Politics and Religion.*

> As America descends deeper into polarization and paralysis, social psychologist Jonathan Haidt has done the seemingly impossible—challenged conventional thinking about morality, politics, and religion in a way that speaks to everyone on the political spectrum...He shows why liberals, conservatives, and libertarians have such different intuitions about right and wrong, and he shows why each side is actually right about many of its central concerns. In this subtle yet accessible book, Haidt gives you the key to understanding the miracle of human cooperation, as well as the curse of our eternal divisions and

> conflicts. If you're ready to trade in anger for understanding, read *The Righteous Mind.*[3]

This knowledge is liberating, and provides guidance for corrective action.

The challenges ahead are global and existential. In order to manage a positive outcome, we need to free ourselves from the forces working to divide us against each other. This will require a step up to a broader sense of group identity and purpose.

Notes

1. Louis Jacobson, *Congress Has 11% Approval Ratings but 96% Incumbent Reelection Rate,* Politifact.com, http://www.politifact.com/truth-o-meter/statements/2014/nov/11/facebook-posts/congress-has-11-approval-ratings-96-incumbent-re-e/ (May 18, 2016).
2. Greg Giroux, *Voters Throw Bums In While Holding Congress in Disdain,* Bloomberg.com, http://www.bloomberg.com/news/articles/2012-12-13/voters-throw-bums-in-while-disdaining-congress-bgov-barometer (May 18, 2016).
3. Haidt, Jonathan. 2012. *The Righteous Mind: Why Good People Are Divided by Religion and Politics.* Random House. New York, NY. Liner notes.

38

Get the Money Out of Politics

In the United States the average Congressman and Senator spends 4-5 hours per day fundraising. In 2012 the average Congressman spent $1.5 million to get elected and the average Senator over $10 million.[1] This money doesn't come without expectations. At a minimum it buys access, and the opportunity to influence policy.

In addition, *Citizens United,* reasoning that corporations are persons and money is speech, has unleashed a torrent of third party money into our political process. Third party spending on political campaigns has soared, from a mere $300,000 in 1978 to over $450 million in 2012.[2] In 2016 one third party network alone is planning to spend almost $900 million,[3] approximately equal to the spending expected for each of the major party presidential campaigns.

A good portion of the third party money, approximately $1 billion total, is expected to be spent on negative ads in

2016.[4] These ads are toxic, profoundly unbalanced at best and often egregiously dishonest. They are not hugely effective in influencing voters,[5] but are very degrading to the process, undermining public confidence in our political system and government, and contributing to the downward spiral of public life.

In addition to direct contributions to candidates and parties, third party money also flows to "think tanks" and lobbyists, who are writing most of the bills these days.[6] "Why are lobbyists writing bills?" you might ask. Because our representatives are busy fundraising from the lobbyists and their financiers, so they don't have time. Also, austerity budgets have resulted in downsizing of legislative staff, so there is not sufficient staff for these tasks. The lobbyists are happy to provide this service for free. Is the resultant legislation likely to be in service to the greatest common good? We report; you decide.

The result of this system is that the people who are successful in running for public office are people who are good fundraisers, and more importantly, who are perceived as willing and able to *deliver value* to their financiers.

This system also has a survivorship bias in favor of people who are willing to work the ethical gray areas, and sometimes even engage in marginally criminal activities, in order to maintain their position in office. A recent news item on a "ski vacation fundraiser"[7]with the Chairman of the powerful House Financial Services Committee highlights the prevailing "ethical standards" surrounding political fundraising. Consider also the "nationwide criminal enterprise"[8] organized by a sitting Governor to finance the defeat of a recall election.

Those who thrive in a corrupted environment are not typically the same people who will spend long hours contemplating and crafting public policy to serve the greatest good, while rejecting partisan pressures.

Those with a genuinely service-oriented character, who are unwilling to participate in such shady practices, are unable to compete given the lopsided resources available to those willing to play ball with influence buyers.

The fact that politics has historically tended to be a dirty business leads many, if not most, to think that nothing can be done about it. But the challenges presented by our technological ascendance will require a more elevated political paradigm if we are to meet them and fashion a positive outcome. *Necessity is the mother of invention.*

We will never have truly honorable process until we get the money out of politics. Over the years there have been numerous efforts at incremental reform, all of which have been ineffective at best, and Citizens United has now blown away any pretense of reasonable limitations. Corporations and the super-rich *do* need to have input into policy decisions, but their avenues for input need to be fully transparent, and balanced with input from the rest of society.

In my opinion, this is an all or nothing issue. If we continue to allow our political process, our representatives and our government to be bought and paid for by deep pocket vested interests, then the political environment will not change, and the penalties we pay as a society will continue to increase.

The elevation to leadership of mature, wise, balanced, pragmatic and genuinely service-oriented people will begin when we create an environment attractive to such people. Better people will create better process. Better process begets better policy, and a more hopeful future.

The path from here to there begins with getting the money out of politics.

Notes

1. Russ Choma, *Election 2012: The Big Picture Shows Record Cost of Winning a Seat in Congress*, OpenSecrets.org, https://www.opensecrets.org/news/2013/06/2012-overview.html (May 18, 2016).
2. Paul Steinhauser and Robert Yoon, *Cost to Win Congressional Election Skyrockets*, CNN.com, http://www.cnn.com/2013/07/11/politics/congress-election-costs/ (May 18, 2016).
3. Matea Gold, *An Amazing Map of the Koch Brothers Massive Political Network*, WashingtonPost.com, https://www.washingtonpost.com/news/the-fix/wp/2014/01/06/mapping-the-koch-brothers-massive-political-network/ (May 16, 2016).
4. Mara Liasson, *Do Political Ads Actually Work?,* NPR.org, http://www.npr.org/sections/itsallpolitics/2012/10/26/163652827/nine-states-near-unlimited-cash-a-flurry-of-ads (May 18, 2016).
5. NPR.org
6. Anthony Madonna and Ian Ostrander, *If Congress Keeps Cutting It's Staff, Who is Writing Your Laws? You Won't Like the Answer*, WashingtonPost.com, https://www.washingtonpost.com/blogs/monkey-cage/wp/2015/08/20/if-congress-keeps-cutting-its-staff-

who-is-writing-your-laws-you-wont-like-the-answer/ (May 18, 2016).

7. Justin Elliot, *House Finance Chair Hensarling Goes on Ski Vacation With Wall Street,* ProPublica.org, https://www.propublica.org/article/house-finance-chair-goes-on-ski-vacation-with-wall-street (May 18, 2016).

8. James Hohmann, *Walker Allegedly in 'Criminal Scheme,'* Politico.com, http://www.politico.com/story/2014/06/scott-walker-campaign-fundraising-108073 (May 18, 2016).

39

Reject the Demagogues

A house divided against itself cannot stand.
—Abraham Lincoln

Most people have limited knowledge of the details, mechanics, nuances, secondary implications, etc. of any particular public policy issue. And very few have a true understanding of the high-level historical forces and economic cycles that precipitate great changes in society and cause periods of economic distress.

The general population depends on civic leaders, journalists and "experts," who are ostensibly better informed, to investigate and inform them of these details.

The current framing of issues by opposing interest groups often runs far astray from anything remotely truthful, causing confusion, and distracting people from the real issues at hand. Ambitious politicians, with the complicity of the media, use these false narratives to gain advantage for themselves and to undermine their opposition.

Demagoguery is the deliberate misrepresentation of information and/or appeal to base emotion—fear, paranoia and scapegoating—for political gain. This practice has become an epidemic in recent years as even the most outrageous lies, distortions and conspiracy theories are widely disseminated on the Internet, and then picked up by the mass media. This coverage legitimizes the distortions, creating widespread confusion about the basic facts of many issues.

The most famous example of demagoguery in recent years was Sarah Palin's characterization of proposed end of life planning as "death panels"[1] in 2009, in an effort to undermine health care reform. End of life planning is a critical non-partisan issue affecting all citizens. If left untended, it creates a great deal of unnecessary suffering and expense for individuals and their families at the end of life, while costing taxpayers billions of dollars a year for unnecessary, and ultimately futile, medical procedures.

Palin's outrageous lie effectively killed any discussion—let alone action—to deal with end of life planning during the drafting of the Affordable Care Act, and the issue was not included in the Act.

Currently, Donald Trump is giving a master class in demagoguery, having vanquished all of his rivals for the 2016 Republican nomination for president, with the most crude, dishonest and divisive campaign in modern times.

More generally, there are many partisan and single-issue

advocacy groups creating division and confusion with their win-at-any-cost tactics.

Typically, there is no compromise or middle ground with these groups. The promoters who consolidate the finances and run the PR campaigns are incentivized to keep the pot boiling. Each side has its own publications and communication networks, which do not speak to each other or acknowledge any validity whatsoever to the opinions of their opposition—ever. They are effectively at war, and as in war, the first casualty is truth.

When we give our support to those who employ such tactics, we are directly contributing to the degradation of public life and the decline of our nation.

When a critical mass generates a cultural imperative for leadership to *transcend* conflict, *solve* the problem at hand, and *resolve* the issues which have given rise to the problem, we can disable the propaganda mills and dis-empower the demagogues.

The truth of the matter is that we *all* have far, far more in common than we have differences.

Notes

1. Angie Drobnic Holan, *Sarah Palin Falsely Claims Barack Obama Runs a 'Death Panel,'* Politifact.com, http://www.politifact.com/truth-o-meter/statements/2009/aug/10/sarah-palin/sarah-palin-barack-obama-death-panel/ (May 18, 2016).

40

Govern the Corporations

An unfortunate feature of modern jurisprudence is the designation of corporations as "persons," with many of the rights of natural persons, but none of the obligations, limitations, loyalties or moral constraints on behavior of natural persons. Recent decisions to extend the rights of corporate persons to include political speech (Citizens United), and religious rights (Hobby Lobby), have made the situation even worse.

Worse yet, in the rare instance when a corporation is found to have committed a crime and actually held accountable to the law, the actual perpetrators of the crime, the executives of the corporation, are not held accountable.

It is the corporation itself that is held accountable, usually in the form of a fine, typically some very small fraction of annual revenues, a penalty paid by the shareholders, not the responsible executives. In effect, corporate officers are for the most part free to do whatever they please without consequence, other than what might be meted out by the corporation internally. It is a setup ripe for abuse, and it *is* abused.

HSBC[1] is an excellent case in point. HSBC was discovered having been laundering money for the Sinaloa drug cartel. These were not the occasional one-off transactions. The arrangement was such that special containers to fill with cash had been manufactured to fit into the drive-in windows at a Mexican branch of the bank. In 2007 and 2008 this HSBC branch transferred over $7 billion to U.S. accounts.

HSBC officials lamented that they would lose $2.6 billion in revenues by closing these accounts. The penalty, $1.9 billion, while a historically large fine, was still considerably less than the illicit gains. The penalty for the responsible officers? They were required to forfeit *some* of their bonuses.

Egregious as the HSBC case is, it is hardly an isolated example. Wachovia Bank[23] was also sanctioned in 2008 for an extensive Mexican money laundering operation, paying a fine of less than 2% of annual profits with no prosecution for any officers involved. Wachovia stock traded up 1% the week the penalty was announced.

Mexican drug cartels launder in the neighborhood of $20-30 billion dollars a year.[4] According to numerous press reports, virtually all of the big multinational banks are complicit. And their criminal activities extend beyond money laundering. In 2015 alone, Citigroup, JPMorgan Chase, Barclays, Royal Bank of Scotland and UBS all paid large fines[5] to settle charges of conspiring to manipulate foreign exchange markets. Deutsche Bank recently admitted to manipulating the precious metals markets and promised to reveal co-conspirators.[6] An entire book could be written on the illegal activities of the banks.

The culture allowing these criminal activities to thrive is endemic in large corporations, not just in the banks. Volkswagon was recently caught in a multi-year cheating scheme to evade emissions standards.[7] General Motors, Fiat Chrysler and Honda all paid big fines for safety violations.[8] Anadarko agreed to pay *$5 billion* to settle charges related to toxic dumping.[9]

These two policies—corporations designated as persons, and lack of accountability of corporate executives—create powerful incentives for corporations to ignore the legal constraints on illicit activities. If they don't get caught, they reap windfall profits from the illegal activity, and if they do get caught, the consequences are minimal. They may have to give up *some* of the ill-gotten gains and no-one goes to jail. It's a win-win. There is no real downside to the corporation *or* the executives for breaking the law.

Corporations are social machines, and like any machine they are value neutral in the abstract. In practice, the values of a corporation are those the managers of the corporation give it. With major incentives encouraging base values and penalties for fine values, the outcome is not hard to predict.

Restoration of balance in our society will require adjustments in corporate policy to eliminate the perverse incentives noted above, and to enhance incentives for good corporate citizenship. We especially need to promote business models that consider the needs of all the stakeholders in the corporate enterprise, including the interests of society as a whole.

If these changes are to yield a net benefit for society, they must and can be instituted without dampening the natural and healthy "animal spirits" that drive innovation and growth. These are not mutually exclusive considerations.

Notes

1. John Burnett, *Awash in Cash, Drug Cartels Rely on Big Banks to Launder Profits*, NPR.org, http://www.npr.org/sections/parallels/2014/03/20/291934724/awash-in-cash-drug-cartels-rely-on-big-banks-to-launder-profits (May 18, 2016).
2. Ed Vulliamy, *How a Big US Bank Laundered Billions From Mexico's Murderous Drug Gangs*, TheGuardian.com, http://www.theguardian.com/world/2011/apr/03/us-bank-mexico-drug-gangs (May 18, 2016).
3. Yves Smith, *Wachovia Paid Trivial Fine for Nearly 0 Billion of Drug Related Money Laundering*, NakedCapitalism.com, http://www.nakedcapitalism.com/2011/04/wachovia-paid-trivial-fine-for-nearly-400-billion-of-drug-related-money-laundering.html (May 18, 2016).
4. NPR.org
5. Phil Mattera, *17 of the Worst Corporate Crimes of 2015*, Alternet.org, http://www.alternet.org/economy/17-worst-corporate-crimes-2015 (May 18, 2016).
6. *Deutsche Bank Admits it Rigged Gold Prices, Agrees to Expose Other Manipulators*, Zerohedge.com, http://www.zerohedge.com/news/2016-04-14/first-silver-now-gold-deutsche-bank-admits-it-also-rigged-gold-prices-legal-settleme (May 18, 2016).
7. Zerohedge

8. Zerohedge
9. Zerohedge

41

Limit the Concentration of Power

> Power tends to corrupt, and absolute power corrupts absolutely. Great men are almost always bad men.
> —*Lord Acton*

A major theme of American conservatives has been their opposition to "big government." This is not an illegitimate concern. Grover Norquist, a "leading light" of the conservative movement once put it like this: "My goal is to cut government in half in 25 years; to get it down to the size where we can drown it in the bathtub."

Cutting the footprint of government in our society in half is probably a good idea, but the desire to "drown it in the bathtub" reveals a pathology infecting a great deal of our public debate.

Such incendiary expressions and appeals to base emotion derail rational debate, and therefore any hope of policy development truly in the common interest. In this case, they completely obscure the real issue, which is not government per se, but the size thereof.

Government is not the enemy. Government is *us*, acting through our elected representatives. But *big* government can become disconnected and deaf to its creators, and the captive of vested interests. Big size, and the concentration of power commensurate with that size is the real issue. And it is not only big government which presents this problem, but big corporations as well.

Big organizations concentrate power, and that power tends to corrupt those who hold the reigns to it.

Big government and big corporations quite naturally fall into a symbiotic relationship, nurturing each other in their quest for ever more power, working together to crush any threats to their position.

Crispin Sartwell, in an Atlantic essay[1] puts forth a *Principle of Hierarchical Coincidence,* which posits that "resources flow toward political power, and political power flows toward resources; or, the power of state and of capital typically appear in conjunction and are mutually reinforcing."

An essential element of the task of restoring balance to our society is the revival of a robust anti-trust effort, and the breakup of the biggest corporations and distribution of their power, concurrent with a downsizing of our dependence on centralized government. There are many industries exhibiting monopoly behavior that need downsizing, so that real competition and economic vitality can be restored: e.g.

airlines, hospitals, health insurance, pharmaceuticals, banking, agriculture, retail and technology.

Big corporations will complain about loss of competitive advantage in the global marketplace. This is a bogus claim. Mammoth corporations are anti-competitive, and they are not necessary to compete for big deals. Syndication will serve nicely for big deals, as it has in the past. Syndication will also promote greater transparency, and therefore more honorable behavior.

Corporations so large that they are "systemically important" cannot be allowed to fail, and therefore it is not possible to hold them accountable for their actions. The rule should be, if it's too big to hold accountable, then it's too big, period. Any such entity needs to shed assets until it's small enough to take to the woodshed, or send its executives to prison, without endangering our economy.

The biggest monopoly of them all is the Federal Reserve, which has taken control of our economy, completely distorting the marketplace, creating massive liabilities that will never be repaid, and effectively expropriating the income and savings of the middle and working classes for the benefit of the very largest financial entities. The final chapter of this ongoing violation has not yet been written. When it is, it will be painful, and it may provide an opportunity to sweep away all the corrupt practices leading to this debacle, once and for all.

Notes

1. Crispin Sartwell, *The Left-Right Political Spectrum is Bogus*, TheAtlantic.com, http://www.theatlantic.com/politics/archive/2014/06/the-left-right-political-spectrum-is-bogus/373139/ (May 18, 2016).

42

Hold Officials Accountable

There has probably not been any single issue that has generated more anger and resentment across the political spectrum than the unequal application of justice.

In an ideal world there would be no need for accountability, because each individual and each group would hold themselves accountable. But we do not yet live in an ideal world. Until we do, we need social and legal mechanisms to hold people accountable for their actions, regardless of their status.

We all strive to maximize our opportunity in life, and that process of striving is naturally driven by incentives. We are incentivized by the satisfaction of a job well done, a new achievement, the recognition of our peers, victory in competition, promotion, material gain. It is the nature of life to grow, and we naturally want to expand our knowledge, achievement and territory of influence. The rewards at each level spur us on.

Sometimes we are tempted to take shortcuts, cheat in competition, or otherwise violate what we know to be honorable behavior in order to gain, to win. None of us is perfect. Just as we need incentives to spur us on in our growth and mastery, we also need incentives to remind us that there is a price to pay for failure to uphold honorable standards.

The average person is generally held accountable to the standards of society—often rather harshly. The U.S. has the dubious distinction of jailing more of its population than any other country—approximately 715 per 100,000[1]—the great majority of them non-violent offenders. The next closest country is Russia at approximately 600 per 100,000. European countries average approximately 100 per 100,000.

However, public and corporate officials are seldom held personally accountable for their actions. The higher the position, the less likely they are to be held accountable—a rather perverse state of affairs. The *highest* standards should be in place for those whose activities have the greatest impact on society, and the most severe consequences should be reserved for those in senior positions who violate those standards.

An important, but little known, fact is that all federal judges take a *separate* oath of office specifically related to this matter.

> I, ________, do solemnly swear (or affirm) that **I will administer justice without respect to persons, and do equal**

> **right to the poor and to the rich**, and that I will faithfully and impartially discharge and perform all the duties incumbent upon me as ________ under the Constitution and laws of the United States. So help me God.[2]

It is hard to square this oath with the unequal application of justice seen in practice.

Notes

1. *Incarceration in the United States*, Wikipedia, https://en.wikipedia.org/wiki/United_States_incarceration_rate (July 27, 2016).
2. *Text of the Oaths of Office of Supreme Court Justices*, SupremeCourt.gov, https://www.supremecourt.gov/about/oath/textoftheoathsofoffice2009.aspx (July 27, 2016).

43

Separate News and Entertainment

> The purpose of journalism is to provide citizens with the information they need to make the best possible decisions about their lives, their communities, their societies, and their governments.[1]
>
> —*The American Press Institute*

A major contributing factor to the devolution of public life in America has been the ascendance of a hybrid form of the news that could be called "newsertainment." As the news media has consolidated into fewer and fewer hands—large corporate hands—the motivation of owners has become less and less about the core purpose and values of the news business, and more about the contribution of the news "division" to the corporate bottom line.

The corporate bottom line is served by maximizing the number of "eyeballs" the media can entice to follow their version of the news. Thus was born "newsertainment," which spins (read: distorts) the daily news to create maximum impact and engagement of viewers by promoting division, conflict and endless drama.

Newsertainment was trail-blazed by talk radio giant Clear Channel, which carved out its market dominance featuring right-wing talk show demagogue Rush Limbaugh. CNN brought us the first live-action war as entertainment—Operation Desert Storm, and the "24 hour news cycle" with its continuous looping of dramatic events, such as the collapse of the World Trade Center towers on 9/11.

Roger Ailes, CEO of Fox News, most clearly perceived the entertainment potential of the news, and led Fox to domination of cable news under its Orwellian banner, "fair and balanced." Ailes turned Fox into the news version of pro wrestling by promoting incendiary headliners and attractive female anchors, and giving extensive coverage to right-wing conspiracy theories. MSNBC joined the fray, attempting to counter Fox from the left, with limited success, and a plethora of on-line outlets have also sprung up to stoke the partisan fires.

These outlets are incentivized to hype breaking news and promote drama at every opportunity. They spin the news daily, often in divisive and incendiary language to provoke base emotion and conflict-based engagement, thus gathering a following for themselves and eyeballs to feed the corporate bottom line. The various outlets have carved up the viewership by spinning their presentations and coverage to suit the predispositions of different segments of the population, liberal or conservative.

This strategy has succeeded in cleaving America in half with an entirely false and dishonest left/right narrative.[2] Viewers are continuously reminded that there is an "us vs. them" dynamic in virtually all issues of general concern.

There have always been marginal media outlets serving social outliers, but the emergence of newsertainment into the mainstream media has been profoundly destructive to national unity, sowing division, distrust and hatred, and promoting the partisan divide that has reached an extreme not seen since the Civil War.[3]

If we expect to have any chance of elevating our society to an honorable political process and towards a more hopeful future, the incentives for large media corporations to profit from distorting the news and promoting conspiracy theories must end.

A major contribution to the transition to the high road will be to break up the media conglomerates, build a firewall between news and entertainment, and apply policy remedies to restore the fundamental purpose and values of the news business.

A good start, and possibly all the policy needed to accomplish this objective, would be the restoration of the Fairness Doctrine (ch. 22, Pragmatism). This move would create a legal battle. News outlets left and right, which have been the major financial beneficiaries of the demise of the

Fairness Doctrine, would howl over the restriction of their free speech, and their right to promote misinformation and conspiracy theories.

But the right to free speech is not unlimited. The example of shouting "fire" in a crowded theater is well known. Also, not so well known, it is against the law to disparage perishable food products or publish child pornography. In these cases there is a demonstrable public harm caused by this speech.

Citizens will need to step up and demand their right to factual and balanced discussion of the issues, so they can make informed decisions on public policy. When they are deliberately misinformed by public media, they are harmed because they are not able to effectively exercise their rights and responsibilities as citizens "to make the best possible decisions about their lives, their communities, their societies, and their governments."

Notes

1. *What is the Purpose of Journalism?,* AmericanPressInstitute.org, https://www.americanpressinstitute.org/journalism-essentials/what-is-journalism/purpose-journalism/ (May 18, 2016).
2. Crispin Sartwell, *The Left-Right Political Spectrum is Bogus*, TheAtlantic.com, http://www.theatlantic.com/politics/archive/2014/06/the-left-right-political-spectrum-is-bogus/373139/ (May 18, 2016).
3. *It's Been 150 Years Since the U.S. Was This Politically Polarized*, Gizmodo.com, http://io9.gizmodo.com/its-been-150-years-since-the-u-s-was-this-politically-1590076355 (June 8, 2016).

44

Renounce Militarism and Empire

It may be difficult to believe, given the daily reports of "wars and rumors of wars," but for most humans the prospect of a violent death is the lowest it has ever been. Steven Pinker has documented the long-term trend toward a more peaceful world in the *The Better Angels of Our Nature: Why Violence Has Declined.*[1]

Despite this hopeful trend, in many parts of the world "politics by other means" still reigns. We need only look at the grinding carnage in Syria to see how bad things can get.

Even in the developed world, the threat of violence hovers in the background, manifesting occasionally as on 9/11, and a spate of recent events in Europe, exacerbated by the flood of refugees from the Middle East.

The modernization of nuclear weapons arsenals, deployments of tactical nukes and missile systems at flashpoints in Eastern Europe and the India-Pakistan border, and nuclear brinksmanship on the Korean Peninsula are increasing the odds of a nuclear conflagration, and a radical disruption in the long downward trend in violent deaths.

The primitive mentality that has created a situation where humanity lives on the knife-edge of annihilation—54 years after the Cuban Missile Crisis—represents a profound failure of political leadership. As new technologies mature and low cost WMDs gradually proliferate, this situation will only get worse, until the worst happens, unless and until we change our thinking.

Until we see "the lion lay down with the lamb" the capability of self-defense remains a necessity for every nation, and the family of nations needs the capacity and the will to respond to such evils as ISIS when they manifest. However, there is a world of difference between national defense and militarism.

During the horrendous global conflicts of the 20th Century, the United States stepped up to turn the tide and prevent global domination, first by Fascism and then by Communism. But the noble response to the moral imperative of defeating totalitarianism gradually morphed into Empire. War-making became an economic strategy, and has remained so in the wake of the collapse of the Soviet Union.

In his Farewell Address,[2] Dwight Eisenhower urged vigilance and readiness to respond to the dark forces in the world should they attempt to harm us. At the same time he warned us to be vigilant of the military-industrial complex, because there were incentives and the potential for these corporate interests to distort national policy and promote wars.

Eisenhower's warning was prescient. The U.S. role of global policeman and enforcer became a reflex action in Washington, where a strong constituency backed by corporate contributions is always ready to unleash U.S. military power on any conflict anywhere in the world. We do need armaments and logistics industries to support our troops, should they be needed. But of all the corporations that need diligent oversight and careful governance, those involved in supplying the implements of war need it most of all.

The truth is that we wage war incessantly because there are scores of corporations making billions of dollars every year supplying and operating our war making machinery (see the top 100),[3] and those corporations spend big to influence public policy.[4]

The U.S. is fatigued from the constant war fighting, and can no longer bear the fiscal burden of more than half of the entire world's military spending.[5]

American military misadventures, from Vietnam to present day disasters in Afghanistan and Iraq, have often proceeded on the thinnest of rationales, with little thought for the long term consequences. In the process the U.S. has squandered trillions of dollars[67] and sacrificed the lives of tens of thousands of its youth,[8] with hundreds of thousands wounded and scarred for life. At the same time it has snuffed out the lives of hundreds of thousands in foreign lands—mostly innocents as in all wars—and destroyed the livelihoods of tens if not hundreds of millions.[910] What has been accomplished with all this violence and bloodshed? Is the world a better place for it? The case can be made that the world is considerably worse off.

The promoters of Empire argue that Empire brings order, and the benefits that flow from order—global trade and a more affluent and relatively peaceful world. At what price?

Given the parabolic increase in technology and the destructive power enabled by that technology, humanity needs to find a better way to promote and support order than by military conquest and subjugation.

America has been the undisputed global hyper-power since the collapse of the Soviet Union in 1991. But the arc of Empire is a historical inevitability, and the U.S. is clearly in decline. America has lost its bearings on the global stage. Its confusion and indecision is apparent globally. Others are rushing to challenge U.S. supremacy, and fill the void it is leaving behind. It is a chaotic and dangerous, but necessary transition.

The U.S. needs to withdraw from Empire and turn inward to resolve its own inner conflicts. America needs some quiet time to reset its moral compass.

Like our bodily defenses, our military should be strong and well supported by industry, but the practical purpose and moral justification for this strong military is for national *defense*, not for imperial conquest.

With the strength and security of a strong national defense, and the resolution of its own inner conflicts, perhaps then America will have the opportunity to demonstrate to the world the benefits of the high road in political process, and create a different kind of Empire, one that the world will not be able to resist, not out of subjugation and fear, but out of inspiration flowing from marvel at the flowering of human potential.

Notes

1. Pinker, Steven. 2011. *The Better Angels of Our Nature: Why Violence Has Declined*. New York, NY. Penguin.
2. *Eisenhower's Farewell Address*, TheAvalonProject,. http://avalon.law.yale.edu/20th_century/eisenhower001.asp, (May 18, 2016).
3. *Top 100 Defense Contractors 2013*, BGA-Aeroweb.com, http://www.bga-aeroweb.com/Top-100-Defense-Contractors-2013.html (May 18, 2016).
4. *Defense*, OpenSecrets.org, https://www.opensecrets.org/industries/indus.php?Ind=D (July 27,2016).
5. *The Real Defense Budget*, Altlantic.com, http://www.theatlantic.com/politics/archive/2012/02/the-real-defense-budget/253327/ (July 28, 2016).
6. Stephen Daggett, *Costs of Major U.S. Wars*, Congressional Research Service, https://www.fas.org/sgp/crs/natsec/RS22926.pdf (September 15, 2016).
7. Neta Crawford, *U.S. Costs of Wars Through 2014: .4 Trillion and Counting*, Boston University, http://watson.brown.edu/costsofwar/files/cow/imce/papers/2014/US Costs of Wars through 2014.pdf (September 15, 2016).
8. *United States Military Casualties of War*, Wikipedia, https://en.wikipedia.org/wiki/United_States_military_casualties_of_war (September 15, 2016).
9. *Vietnam War Casualties*, Wikipedia, https://en.wikipedia.org/wiki/Vietnam_War_casualties#Deaths_caused_by_the_American_military (September 15, 2016).

10. *Casualties of the Iraq War*, Wikipedia, https://en.wikipedia.org/wiki/Casualties_of_the_Iraq_War (September 15, 2016).

45

Attend to the Process

Good process creates good product.

Good process in service to public policy and governance involves communication, research, debate, education, assessment of public needs, desires and resources, crafting of policy and follow up. It includes absorbing inputs, listening to feedback, assessment of results and adjustment of policy. And it requires honest, balanced input from constituents and business interests.

Good political process is consuming and sublime, requiring total absorption by dedicated public servants. Fundraising as a primary, or even secondary, focus of our representatives completely disables the possibility of good process.

Presently, our political process is like an ecosystem overwhelmed by pollution. If the source of the pollution is removed, the force of nature will begin to re-assert itself and the system will soon begin to function normally.

Relentless scorched earth partisan warfare has neutered our political process, and brought our system of governance to a standstill. Jimmy Carter recently noted that at present, America doesn't have a functional democracy.[1]

Good process is not difficult to envision. At a minimum it requires respectful and honest debate, and an environment supportive of genuinely service-oriented candidates. This will require dismantling incentives for politicians, advocacy groups and media to promote and benefit from misinformation and conflict, while establishing procedures, resources and incentives to transcend conflict and promote honest debate.

Political process is like a garden; it yields a new crop every season. If we create a cultural imperative to support and safeguard an honorable process in service to the greater good, we can rest assured that each new crop will be nourishing and life supporting. At the same time, like a garden, we will need to be vigilant to encroachment of negative influences (weeds) and pull them early before they take over.

Policy will resolve itself over time if we put our process in order, and tend to it as a matter of civic responsibility.

Notes

1. Eric Zuesse, *Jimmy Carter is Correct That the U.S. is No Longer a Democracy*, HuffingtonPost.com, http://www.huffingtonpost.com/eric-zuesse/jimmy-carter-is-correct-t_b_7922788.html (May 18, 2016).